WHAT OTHERS ARE SAYING

Nothing is quite as disparaging for the entrepreneur than creating that amazing product that we are certain the whole world needs only to have a dismal response...ok, NO response (except from your mom and two best friends). The big problem is usually NOT the most obvious. In this book, Darlene gives us an action plan for the remedy-- creating that "Nectar effect." I love it! This book is a keeper. In fact, it is the book that covers the missing secret to success that so many entrepreneurs have been missing and crying out for. This is certainly a book that will meet you wherever you are and take you uplevel in your business. Apply **"The Nectar Effect"** *and you will find yourself building that profitable, productive, and very successful business that you only dared to dream about!*

Cindy Rushton, The Biz Mentor, www.TheBizMentor.com

Many are called to entrepreneurship but few are chosen because of natural ability. What if you could present, promote and prosper as yourself with the assistance of a serial entrepreneur who has spent the hours and dollars so you don't have to suffer unprofitable overwhelm? **The Nectar Effect** *is simple wisdom for the complex formula to business success.*

Latosha Jenkins www.YourBottomLineRealtors.com

The Nectar Effect *is the one business-motivational book that will show you the only success element that you possess and no one else does - yourself. People scramble around looking for that one magical way to attract their target market to their business; many even pay top dollar for it. In reality, the one edge you have over anyone else is your own flair, your own uniqueness, and your own "Nectar." What a relief to know that you already have everything you need to attract the kind of people you seek out, and for those of us who just might need a gentle reminder of how to use what we've got, Darlene and Polly walk us through the steps. You'll find countless tried-and-true suggestions, expert advice, and logical solutions all delivered with a smile and a fun-loving, peaceful spirit.* ***The Nectar Effect*** *is bound to draw out the best t*hat's *already within you; give yourself the chance.*

Sharon Larson www.SharonTogether.com

I will tell you point blank that I am not a hustler. Something about giving a sales pitch makes me feel dirty inside. That's why this book is so perfect. It lovingly and effectively points out that small business isn't about schmoozing; it's about relationship building with human beings.

I recently co-founded a publishing company despite my natural allergies to dealing with money. Reading ***The Nectar Effect*** *has pointed out several areas in which I innately excel, but it also points out some major blind spots. I will definitely be using the knowledge I gained from* *this book to further develop my business. Many of the ideas presented are invaluable to any small business.*

So why are you still reading this? Buy the book, already! Turn your business from drab to fab.

Ditrie Sanchez www.spectaclepmg.com

*With **The Nectar Effect**, Darlene and Polly have captured the essence of what modern marketing is all about – the steady drip of tantalizing contact. This book examines a variety of ways that small business people can create desire in the mind of customers and prospects, and keep them coming back for more. It should come as no surprise that the flower's sweet Nectar, and more importantly how insects respond to it, are in fact the perfect metaphor for brand marketing and consumer behavior. That said, this book is about far more than clever alliteration, and concrete strategies and tactics abound. **The Nectar Effect** provides a great springboard for anyone intent on learning to market themselves and their brand.*

Ben Robbins www.VeniceExperiment.com

The Nectar Effect
*Be Irresistible and Attract
What you Want in Your Business*

No part of this publication may be reproduced, stored in a retrieval system, or transmitted, in any form, or by any means, electronic, mechanical, photocopying, recording, or otherwise, without the prior consent of the publisher.

Note: For the purpose of full disclosure, some of the links in this book provide the author with a commission or other benefit. The author never recommends what Ishe doesn't already use or have personal experience with.

The author is not responsible for either the content or output of the links inside this book leading to external websites. At the time of publication all links were working, but business owners change their websites from time to time which can make the links in this book obsolete or cause them to lead to a different page than was originally intended.

PLEASE READ CARFULLY:
Any content, information, and any materials provided in this message is on an as is basis. The author makes no warranty, expressed or implied, as to its accuracy, completeness or timeliness. Neither are any promises of results to be obtained by the recipients, implied. The author shall not, in any way, be liable to any recipient for any inaccuracies, errors or omissions herein.

Cover Design: Tina Hull, Khymera Design, www.KhymeraDesign.com

Author photo: Alexandra Chubachi, Alexandra Danae Photography

Copyright 2014 Darlene Hull

ISBN: 978-0-9917947-3-7

For the struggling home and small business owner everywhere:

You have the dream

You have the determination

You have the discipline

May these tools be the key that unlocks your success

And for Alice Wheaton for long walks, deep conversations, and for working so hard for to make me look good!

The Nectar Effect

*Be Irresistible and Attract
What you Want in Your Business*

By
Darlene Hull
and
Polly Mayforth Krause

HotSpot Publishing
Calgary, AB

Contents

1. How to use this book 13
2. A Sweet Introduction 15
3. The Right Gardening Tools 21
4. Up Close and Personal 31
5. The Customer is Gold 43
6. Pick Up the Phone 55
7. Schmoozing on Social Media 67
8. The Magic of a Greeting Card 83
9. A Little Gift to Remember Me By 97
10. Creating a Stir Through Events 105
11. Trade Show Tactics 113
12. Conclusion 125
    Acknowledgements 127
    About the Authors 129

HOW TO USE THIS BOOK

This book introduces 8 different ways to market your business. You don't need to read them in any particular order, but we highly recommend you begin with the first 3 chapters so you have the proper foundation for the application of the different marketing ideas provided. Once you've read the first 3 chapters, feel free to bounce around the different chapters at will.

If you scan through this book you'll notice that it is filled with QR codes that look something like this:

HotSpot Social Media

If you're not familiar with them, these codes are meant to be scanned with your smartphone using a scanning app which is usually free to download. Check this website for a list of scanners you can choose from: QR.TheNectarEffect.com. Scanning these codes is almost like taking a picture, but the phone does the clicking when the code is in focus. Once you've scanned the code you will be taken to the website that is indicated. This enables you to read further or check out any of the links and websites offered without having to type in

The Nectar Effect

the URL. Once you scan a code it stays in your phone like a photo in the scanning app, and you can return to it at any time.

Of course, you can also access the sites via the shortened URLs provided if you'd rather not download another app.

We recommend having your phone beside you as you read so you can follow the links for more information.

We hope you enjoy the book!

A Sweet Introduction

One of the most beautiful, but underestimated flowers is the is the daisy. Their simple, sunny faces remind me that life and success don't need to be complicated. There is often great beauty in simplicity. Like all other flowers, daisies aren't hoping to get by on their good looks alone. They have a sweet secret that helps them grow, flourish, and spread; it's called Nectar. Bees use it to make the golden, delicious honey we spread on our toast and spoon into our tea. The bee gains the gold, and the plant has the joy and opportunity to reproduce for one more day.

What does all this flowery language have to do with you and me? Well, you could say, the flower is one of the best marketers on earth and we human beings ought to take more than an appreciative glance. Entrepreneurs, employers and employees, those who are wealthy and those who wish to be, are all marketers. Whether we offer a product or a passel of skills, we must sell to survive and for those of you who would rather eat raw liver than try to convince someone that they want something, this truth simply sucks. How do we, the less flashy flowers in the plot, go about getting the loving we need not just to survive, but to thrive?

This book delivers good news for those who hate the idea of pushing themselves forward for the sake of a sale! The Internet has made it possible for you to put yourself and your product in front of billions of people in ways that are non-terrifying or awkward.

The Nectar Effect

You don't need office space, employees or an espresso machine. You don't need expensive airtime on the tube - because we all know that commercials are like elevator muzak, the background track to the bathroom dance or putting another load through the washing machine! You don't need a front page advert in the local newspaper. Best news of all, you don't need a massive billboard featuring an artificial sex goddess selling your product. You don't need to be a jolly talk-show host or have the jam to sell umbrellas in a drought. There are simple steps you can take to set yourself up for success.

For starters, grab an inexpensive laptop from your local computer emporium and belay the net, but bear in mind that you're hanging at ground zero. Yes, you'll want to focus considerable time and effort on the web, but don't discount the importance of your family, friends and community. You need a place to grow your skills where people already know, trust and love you. They'll help you bloom to the point where your Nectar will be evident even on a 2D screen. If you plan to jump ahead to the "How-To" sections on marketing, you'll be missing the buzz. You don't have to be an expert to auto-tweet and thoroughly exasperate the good people of this planet! (Did you know that repeated exasperation can lead to anger, or worse, apathy? This is NOT a great marketing technique!) You may already have a bustling Facebook page and a hip Twitter account. You may already be dropping carefully crafted teasers on your friends and followers. Are you achieving the results you want? If the answer is no, it's the Nectar that's missing. You need to begin by recognizing it in yourself and releasing it's perfume wherever you are.

It was a glorious morning - blue sky, green grass, flowers displaying their wares in a colourful array. My spirit was light, my heart was singing as I walked along. I was about to pass an older woman and I gave her a bright smile and a cheery good morning! She nodded, walked past, stopped and walked back, and tapped me on the shoulder.

"Excuse me," she asked; "Do I know you?"

A Sweet Introduction

I explained that I'd never seen her before, but that it was such a beautiful day, I couldn't help but spread my joy. She was surprised, and she smiled as she went on her way.

Isn't it sad that a happy hello could cause such a curious reaction? Why did this woman approach me rather than continuing on her obviously un-merry way? She stopped because of the Nectar. She stopped because openness and warmth are attractive. Do you remember the stories your grandparents used to tell about that quaint small town experience where you knew every one of the folks who strolled by, and if you didn't know them, you offered your hand before they could lift their eyes to yours. We now live in a society where we are increasingly isolated due to busy schedules, fear of strangers, and mechanization. Add the virtual world of cyberspace to the burden and it's no wonder people marvel at the applied heat of human kindness. We're more connected than ever, and at the same time, more isolated.

The people around us, the people plugged up with earphones paying more attention to their tiny screens than to the fascinating people around them don't know it, but what they want - what they need - from you isn't necessarily your product, it's your Nectar. It's so easy to hide behind all our gadgets, but hiding won't get us the validation we're longing for. We desperately want to be seen and known.

What is the Nectar? The Nectar is uniquely you. The Nectar is that goodness present in all of us. Everyone has some sparkling quality, some startling intelligence or some exceptional skill to share. What is your special sweetness, the essence of you that you reserve for your mother, your children, your lover? Get it out there! Be yourself with every person you stumble upon and view them as gifts worth opening and appreciating. Don't do it because you're desperate to make a sale. Do it because you're a caring, compassionate person. Do it because you're a social dynamo who wants to connect on a deeper level. Even if you're a bit shy, there are ways to safely emerge from the wallpaper.

The Nectar Effect

Let's go back to the basics, the lessons we thought we learned from our moms and dads and grandmas and grandpas that we can no longer find in the kerfuffle of our adult minds.

Irresistibility Tips:

Bee Polished: You don't have to have teeth the colour of a virgin snow or be really, really, really good looking in the immortal words of Derek Zoolander, but you do need to spice up what you've been given. Put your best face and foot forward. Slovenliness will get you nowhere except maybe a permanent seat on the old couch.

Some of you might not want to hear this, but if, like me, you have the fashion sense of a duck, you may have to relearn how to dress yourself. As a professional, not only do our clothes need to be crisp and clean, they need to work for the bodies and colouring we currently have. Some people have the knack, some people don't. Whether you like it or not, first impressions count! Remember, a shine on your shoes is a smile on your feet!

Bee Confident: You're looking good. Now manifest that in the way you carry yourself. Hold your head up, walk with purpose and look people in the eye. Develop a firm, but friendly handshake. Learn to smile! The sincere smile is really the avatar of the Nectar. Remember, too, it's not only about the mouth, but about the eyes. People can finger a fake and you'll have to work that much harder to gain their trust if you fake your smile.

Bee Considerate: Use your manners. Please and thank you are two of the most effective expressions in the human language and can't be overused like the word sorry (we Canadians are bad for this). Using please and thank you communicates respect and humility. Don't stop there. Be on the alert for opportunities to assist others. Open doors, offer aid when you see someone struggling to load something into their vehicle; don't be so set in your schedule that you're not able to help a Joe or Jane who has the courage to ask you for a favour.

A Sweet Introduction

Take advantage of any and every encounter with others. Connect whenever possible. It's called kindness and it should be lavished on others intentionally, liberally and creatively every day.

Bee Present: This is important. When the people you're with - friends new and old - see that you're distracted by looking around, checking your cell phone, asking them to repeat themselves, etc., they will begin to feel you're not interested in them and distance will be created that you'll have to bridge to continue the relationship. Your friends will be more forgiving than your acquaintances, but even they'll get tired of the lack of reciprocity. Unless you're a medical doctor or your children need to contact you in case of an emergency, keep the pocket phone turned off in your pocket. We know this will be hard for some of you, but wouldn't we all love to think that we are the most important person in the room to the person we're speaking with?

Bee Genuine: You've done the work of sprucing up the package, you're minding your manners and you're giving of yourself, but all that is just bling if your soul is a grasping, shriveled, lonely pea. If you're serious about making the jump to personal super stardom, you have to find your authentic self and live from it. Go ahead. Laugh at this, mock it for being sentimental schlock, but there will be no Nectar, no irresistible magnetic pull and no return if you don't know who you are and what you want. Your confusion concerning this matter will, yes, confuse people and detract from the confident, intelligent, stable person you're busily building. There are plenty of self-help books, gurus to lead you on the path to enlightenment, supportive groups, family and friends to cheer you on, a higher power to hold on to and gain strength and hope from, if you choose. However you decide to grow yourself, I encourage you to get on with it. Only those who have accepted their brokenness, named their strengths and are interested in reaching their potential will be effective at freeing their Nectar and meeting the needs of others and themselves in the most life-giving, profound way.

The Nectar Effect

Bee memorable: If you've completed the list and you've committed yourself to working on that last often painful process, this "Bee" should be taken care of, but it's worth emphasizing.

Endless Referrals

In his book *Endless Referrals* (ER. NectarEffect.com) - a book I HIGHLY recommend - Bob Burg tells the story of how a cell phone salesman, in the days before cell phones were believed to be as necessary as oxygen, kept up a relationship with him in the hopes that one day Bob would buy a phone from him. Bob assured the salesman that if the time came, this salesman would get the call. The time came through an emergency situation with Bob's parents. Suddenly Bob was in a panic to purchase a phone. He grabbed the Yellow Pages, called a company and bought a phone. Only after the crisis was averted, did he remember the salesman. Bob felt terrible. He called the salesman and confessed, apologizing profusely.

It's not enough to be known, liked and trusted. You have to be *remembered*. You need to make an irreversible imprint, a branding, so to speak.

At the end of the day, it's all about the Nectar. You can have the best quality product, but unless you can attract and secure peoples' business over and over and over again, your success will be diluted

Next up? The step-by-step for building connections that lead to business. Mark my words, however, if you've ignored this chapter, the following techniques won't work as well for you. Techniques without the essence of genuine personality and style are dry and lifeless. Just as there is little Nectar in flowers that grow in dry, rocky soil, there is no Nectar in empty techniques.

You have been warned.

The Right Gardening Tools

Congratulations for embarking on the journey of a lifetime. If you've primed your presentation and you're working on growing your soul, then it's time to look at how to apply your authentic, irresistible self to your business.

You can choose to slam your way into the crowd like a lineman intent on taking the quarterback down - and certainly giving your best is encouraged – but know that in business your time, resources, and finances are limited. You need to make sure you send your Nectar to the ones out there who are specifically looking for it.

Once you've cared for yourself and your family, it's time to face the requirements for growing your business. You need to start by assembling your gardening tools.

Gardening Tools:

Define your target market. Spend your energy and efforts winning over those people who are going to get the most benefit both from a relationship with you and a great experience of your product or service. Somewhere out there is a group of people that you relate well to, that you enjoy spending time with and with whom you have a lot in common. In that group of people there is hopefully a sub-set of people who are as hungry for your product as a bee is for Nectar. Now you may be selling something as common as toothpaste, something that everyone needs, wants, and can benefit from. The problem is if you try and reach everyone, you'll be broke long before you make enough sales to cover your business costs. It

The Nectar Effect

Target Market

feels counter-intuitive to narrow your field rather than expand it, but here's the truth: the more targeted your market is, the more you're able to channel your energy into understanding that particular segment of society. This understanding enables you to become an expert for that community, thus becoming the go-to person for toothpaste. If you do a brilliant job of that, word will spread and you'll find people from outside that market coming to you and saying things like "I know I'm not a mom of a toddler (your target market), but I'm part of a group of bankers who I think would be really into your toothpaste. Do you think you could sell us toothpaste as well?" Your market expands naturally if you do a fabulous job of the market you focus on (see our worksheet on Target Markets here: http://Target.HotSpotSocialMedia.com if you need help with this).

You shouldn't just latch onto any old sub-set if you want to be wildly successful. There are certain criteria you need to keep in mind:

1. You should already be in contact with your chosen target market, or at least able to be regularly in contact with them in some kind of natural fashion, in order to connect well and build the trust that is so important to repeat sales.

2. The sub-set you choose must be able to afford your services or product.

3. There must be enough people in that sub-set to make it possible for you to earn a comfortable living, however you define that, without spending 20 hours a day, seven days a week, making it happen.

4. Determine at least 2-3 factors that distinguish this group. In other words, don't pick "Mothers" as your sub set. Pick "overweight, busy mothers" for example.

The Right Gardening Tools

When that's done, run this by a couple of trusted friends to see if it makes sense. For example, if – as mentioned above *overweight mother of toddlers* is your chosen ideal client and you're selling a diet system that requires eating specific food at regular intervals 5-6 times a day and doing two 40-minute uninterrupted sessions of specialized fitness, you might need to re-adjust to *overweight stay-at-home moms of kids in preschool or daycare*. See what I mean? Your specialized sub-group has to fit your product or service. Once you've chosen your ideal sub-set of people you need to drill down one more step.

Your Instinctual Client

When bees are searching for Nectar they aren't going after every single flower in the vicinity. No they are looking for some specific criteria: the flowers must be sweetly scented, the Nectar itself must be easy to obtain – like in a rose, rather than a chrysanthemum – and it must have a comfortable "landing pad" so the bee has a place to rest while gathering the Nectar.

Just like the bee, you are looking for specific traits in the people you will be presenting your product to. Somewhere in that group of people you've chosen as your target market is a certain kind of person to whom you are naturally drawn; a certain kind of someone you automatically relate to, who is also a person who both needs and *desires* what you have to offer, and to whom offering your product or service is as natural as tying your shoes. This is your instinctual client.

Take time to enter into the subset you've chosen to identify this instinctual client. What's her name? Her family situation? Where does she work and what's her income? How does she spend her free time? Her discretionary cash? Ideally, you give her a name, a face, a life.

Now, when you're going about your day and someone comes to you bearing the description that you pre-formulated, you've identified your first prospect. The more you know about her, the better you can connect with her and serve her.

The joy of having figured out who your target market is ahead of time is that you now only do business in places where these ideal clients hang out, whether online or offline. If your ideal client isn't at your local networking group, neither are you. If your local client doesn't play golf, don't buy a membership thinking it will pump up your pocketbook. Spend your time where your ideal client is. Place your ads in publications that your ideal client reads. Join online groups your ideal client is involved in. See the magic? No more running crooked and tossing your cash helter-skelter in all directions. Specialize to maximize.

Your Nectrified Sweet Spot

If you're going to build a relationship with this special person, you have to know how to connect to them in a way that creates a positive response. You need to know their needs, their problems and frustrations. How does what you offer alleviate their pain? How do you come alongside and ease that frustration? What are the specific benefits of your product that will enhance person's lifestyle?

Perhaps you offer protein shakes for quick weight loss. The benefits for your instinctual client is they can eat what they want for dinner, no need to make separate meals for the family, they're already pre-measured, no counting calories or weighing food and they're portable. Add the fact that they're incredibly affordable to the list so that the stay-at-home mom doesn't need to blow her grocery budget to pay for them, and you're ready to make the next step. It's time to create a "Unique Selling Proposition" or USP. This is a short, catchy phrase not unlike the subtitle of a book, that answers

USP

your instinctual client's need. It's purpose is to create the effect that you are calling your client by name even when they are a stranger to you:

"No fuss, no mess, no worries; weight loss solutions for busy moms."

This phrase will appear under your company name on your business card and printed materials. If you need help with it, we have a worksheet on that, too:

http://USP.HotSpotSocialMedia.com

Your Nectar Dripping Pitch

Next, expand your catch phrase to include more detail about your product/service. This is destined to become the response you give people when they ask the ubiquitous question "What do you do?" There's a wonderful book on this topic by Kim Klaver called *If My Product's So Great How Come I Cant Sell It?* (http://KK.TheNectarEffect.com/) where the author provides the steps to writing a Nectar Dripping Pitch. She takes a lot of time to explain the how and why if that's important to you. Otherwise for the sake of brevity, we'll move on to a quick and easy formula:

Kim Klaver

1. **Tell us what you do in its simplest form: For example:** "*I market a meal replacement product...*"

2. **Identify the negative emotions your ideal client is experiencing, the "pain" and frustration" we mentioned above. For example:** "*...for busy, overweight...*"

3. **Identify your ideal client:** "*moms*"

4. **Name your solution:** "*...that adds no mess, fuss or worries to their already hectic schedules..."*
5. **List 3 benefits to your client:** "*...This product enables moms to easily lose weight without experiencing hunger or complicating their lifestyle...*"
6. **Ask for the sale** "*Do you know anyone who might be helped by this?*"

Combine the pieces and play with it until it clicks.

> *I market a meal replacement product for busy, overweight moms that adds no mess, fuss or worries to their already hectic schedules. This product enables moms to easily lose weight without experiencing hunger or complicating their lifestyle. Do you know anyone who might benefit from this?*

Keep playing with your unique selling proposition until it feels natural, and then memorize it so it's always ready.

Now that you have your gardening tools in place you need to know how to approach this ideal target market. There are 4 keys to effective relationship marketing. Before we get into them, please let me reiterate one more time, you can't fake this.

Robotically mowing through a series of techniques isn't going to be effective. Practise the steps, allowing your Nectar to unfold as you go. Your client's best interest, with or without your product, has to be the motivation. The words "I love you" can be expressed a million ways, but we all know when they come from the heart and when they're frosting on an already gooey cake. Your being must be alive with care and concern for the person you're talking to. This tender attentiveness will be felt by anyone you're involved with and it's an attractive quality.

For those of you who are more reserved, or who struggle with shyness, know that care and concern can be learned. I am very pragmatic. I

The Right Gardening Tools

like lists and schedules. I've raised independent children because I'd sooner push them from the nest, ready to take on the world, than warm them under my wing. It used to be that when I met people with problems, my reflexive response was "suck it up". Though, I sure did appreciate *their* sympathy when *I'm* was suffering! I am innately and selfishly independent, but I've worked hard to tap into and distribute my own Nectar, and I'm here to tell you that you no longer have to be boxed in by your current personality traits.

Fortunately, I'm surrounded by family and friends who are compassionate, kind, considerate, thoughtful and thankful. They used to irritate me. Over time, I've come to realize owning these qualities gave me meaningful, joy-filled days. I've made a point of rubbing up against these sweet, loving people to develop the habit of kindness and to grow a compassionate heart. At first it felt uncomfortable, like any new habit, but I'm happy to report there are those on the planet who have no idea that I'm really a recovering, crusty, old troll. Give your heart room to expand. The sooner you start, the better off you'll be.

The Four Keys

1. **Look and listen.** Pay attention to the people around you: your spouse, children, parents, siblings, friends, the store clerk, the cashier, the barista, the gas jockey, your co-workers. Reflect on what their lives are like. Mark the lines on their faces, note the colour of their eyes, analyze their sense of style, listen to their conversations. What can you learn about a person just from observation? Identify 5 distinct characteristics about each person you see and make this a habit. You'll be surprised at what you learn. Then, describe that person in one word: Vivacious, Introspective, Quirky, Serious, Intense, etc.

2. **Identify Issues.** Ask yourself, if after reviewing your observations, you are able to identify possible issues. Does their face look drawn or pinched? Maybe they're worried or

angry? Do their worn clothes suggest their financial status? By their language or demeanour, do they appear uneducated? Are they overweight? Obviously sick?

Ask yourself why? What could be causing this person pain? Put yourself in their shoes, however smelly they may be. Imagine any such times in your life. The purpose of this exercise is not to pass judgment or patronize people. The purpose is to remind you that you are one of many, and that these are people first, prospects second. The purpose is to raise your awareness that people are struggling and hurting around you and to imbue you with understanding and empathy.

3. **Create and connect.** Start by greeting them. A simple "Hello. How are you today?" is enough to start a conversation. Often, they'll play the game by answering your question and volleying back. We're all socialized enough to trot out the weather, sports, community events etc. You don't have to win a toastmaster's prize for wit and delivery; just connect.

4. **Encourage and empower.** Once you've made the connection, make it a blessing. My Dad is gifted in this respect. He can go into any shop or public place and have the person beside him laughing. He engages everyone from the waitress to the boss. He is quick to say thank you and readily acknowledges terrific service.

Think about how you can offer this person relief or encouragement. Is someone constantly sneezing? Offer a tissue if they don't seem to have a fresh one handy or share a remedy you've found that works for you or a friend. Is someone struggling with a load? Offer to carry packages. Is the person next to you overweight? Pick out an attractive attribute or piece of clothing and compliment them on it. These people get more than their share of judgmental stares.

The Right Gardening Tools

The only difference between you and them is that your weakness probably hides itself better. There's a soul in there and kind words are appreciated by everyone. Break the taboo of silence and try to make everyone you meet feel good about themselves.

At our local library, which we frequent on a weekly basis, there is a clerk who dresses with flair. She always looks fantastic. One day as she was checking out my books I said, "I just need to tell you that you are a beautiful woman and have a tremendous sense of style." She's not a client of ours, never will be, but she's a human being who takes care of herself and takes pride in her looks. It's a joy for me to see her every time. And let me assure you, I never have any issues at her counter with my books. If I need anything, I only have to ask this woman and she goes out of her way to help me. It took very little effort on my part to praise her and because I expended this small amount of energy, she always remembers me.

Practice these four steps wherever you go until they become a part of who you are. There is little to no risk involved in showing kindness. Even if the person does not accept your words or your offers to help, you have lost nothing and may never see them again. The win is so enormous once you establish this practice in your life that it's well worth the temporary discomfort.

You can adopt all the marketing strategies in this book and apply them systematically, but until you're able to make a deep, valid connection with another human being, until you're able to sell yourself in all your unique, sincere glory regardless of what your product or service is, you will fail to progress as quickly as you'd like. You needn't be perfect to get started, just aware. Get started on these traits, and

90 Seconds or Less

remind yourself that just a 1% improvement is enough to create a landslide of change!

If you really feel your people skills are lacking I would highly recommend the book *How to Make People Like You in 90 Seconds or Less* by Nicholas Boothman (http://90.TheNectarEffect.com). Make it a game to tackle one technique every week and see where it takes you.

Continue to work on your social skills as you forge ahead. You'll see that each chapter deals with a certain kind of marketing - face to face, social media etc. At the close of each chapter, you'll find suggestions, an assignment if you will, of tactics you can do *right now*. It is a good idea to apply something you've learned before going on to the next chapter. At the end of our time together, you'll be that much further along the road to success. It's not knowledge that's power, it's *applied* knowledge!

As we move into the practical sections of the book, allow me to offer this advice from Mary Kay Ash:

Pretend that every single person you meet has a sign around his or her neck that says, "Make me feel important."

Up Close and Personal

Not only will you succeed in sales, you will succeed in life. In my family, we have one extrovert and three serious introverts. The extrovert is my son and if it weren't for him, we would not lay eyes on each other, choosing, instead, to communicate via computer. Of the introverts, I am the most accomplished at hiding myself away. I'm painfully shy and every group of people I find myself in makes me feel like I'm a 12-year-old in a gathering of PhD's. Thankfully, my mother, a socialite from a family of socialites, taught me how to handle myself in a crowd. Because of her modeling and tutoring, very few people would describe me as being shy.

Unfortunately, for us introverted types, the most powerful form of marketing is still about physical presence. Inhabiting space and time, looking into each others' eyes, talking and listening, reading body language cues are all vitally important. This is how connections are made and how they grow and flourish. The amount of information you can gain about someone online can't begin to compare to what you can glean by being in the same room with them; this is the ideal. Do whatever you can to get out and connect face-to-face. It's by far the easiest place to deliver the Nectar. Just as bees aren't going to be getting much Nectar from flowers in a picture, your connections are only going to be able to see a very small part of your personality via a computer screen. I've been coaxing myself lately to regularly attend various meetings and events around the city, and to invite people to meet me for coffee to chat about their business and see if there's any way we can collaborate. Through these casual get-togethers, I've developed some very positive connections. If a timid hermit like me can do it, there's hope for all of us! Why not stop now to set up your first meeting? Make your request friendly, but clear, and whatever you do, don't allow them to show up thinking it's a casual drink or a blind date and then whip out your hairnet for a product demo! Be clear on your purpose for the meeting – if you want to share your business opportunity, say that. Don't pretend your interest is all about what they do, when really, all you're going to do is let them talk long enough for you to earn the right for a sales pitch.

Once they've agreed to meet you, make sure you meet in a place you're familiar with where you feel relaxed; preferably one that's tasteful and bright where you won't have to shout at each other.

Mackay 66

Before your meeting do your new friend the honour of researching them to find as many points of connection as possible. Tom Hopkins, sales trainer, created a questionnaire that he used to research his prospects called the Mackay66. It's a series of 66 questions that cover just about any topic you might discuss, many of which can be answered with the help of the Internet. His goal was to have an answer to all of these questions for each of his clients. You will find a copy of this questionnaire, as well as some excellent sales tools, here: http://66.TheNectarEffect.com. Why not have some of these questions in mind when you're chatting with your new contact to help keep the conversation lively and engaging?

Remember to respect their time and be punctual. Commit a heinous abuse of someone else's time and you've just wasted your own as well.

Up Close and Personal

Make a point of using people's names. How often do you hear your name said? Hardly ever, right? But, when you do, you like the sound of it, don't you? We all do. Tap into this tiny need. Don't allow yourself to fall back on the silly excuse that you can't remember names. Take a course to train yourself in this all-important area. When you're introduced to someone, repeat their full name back to them. Ask them how they spell it. Connect their name to some interesting quality about themselves "John Smith the Carpenter" for example. Then in your conversation together, use their name two or three times. Try and introduce them to someone else at your gathering and when you get home, immediately follow up.

People love to talk about themselves. Ask plenty of open ended questions, the kind that require thoughtful exposition. Closed questions, the kind that illicit one word answers that thud to the ground like bricks and echo in the awkward silence between you, must be avoided. When they answer, listen to their responses and take mental notes. Don't interrupt and don't one-up them. Come away from that conversation with details. What's the name of Great Uncle Edward's half-blind seeing eye dog? Where did the she procure that pair of kicky pink heels? Write that information down! You never know when such small things will pay big dividends

Develop referral relationships. Be on the lookout for ways you can send business to your friends. Give your contacts notice that, Mr. Pronk, golfer and great lover of cinnamon toothpicks, may stop by. The more you help grow their business, the more likely they are to reciprocate.

Don't end the friendship because they don't buy the first time - why would you do this? We all need friends. They're as important if not more important than chocolate and it pains me to say this. Keep these statistics from the National Sales Executive Association in mind:

- 2% of sales are made on the 1st contact
- 3% of sales are made on the 2nd contact

The Nectar Effect

- 5% of sales are made on the 3rd contact
- 10% of sales are made on the 4th contact
- *80% of sales are made on the 5th-12th contact* (emphasis mine)

Did you read the stats above without registering the significance? The Nectar is the key. You have to be so genuine, so pleasant, so helpful that your client will want to see you at least 12 times. If all you do is hawk your product when you're together, you'd better have one knockout product or you'll be slobbering on the mat after the first bell.

As I watch my Twitter stream flow by or scan my Facebook page, the things that speak to me are not the ramped up cheerleader come-ons or the undecipherable links. The marketing that draws me in is that which recognizes me as a human being with needs, wants and desires. It gives expression to the value I have as a person, not just as a consumer. I'm more willing to unpack my plastic if I believe the person taking the payment sees me as more than a perpetual string of dollar signs.

Here are more ideas to help you pass on your Nectar to your potential clients and connections. Some of these were touched on in the last chapter, but let me give you some very practical tips here for turning those ideas into actual events:

1. **Find a reason to give a compliment:** Wherever you are, whatever you're doing, be gracious, thoughtful, and encouraging. Are you at the checkout? Compliment the cashier on something - their smile, their pleasant manner, their efficiency, their fashion sense. Be sure to thank them for their assistance when you're done. Are you walking down the street? Look people in the eye as you pass, smile, and praise the weather, admire their outfit, comment on how adorable their dog is.

Up Close and Personal

2. **Start a conversation**: In a waiting room? Often it's obvious who is willing to make conversation as they're already talking. Take a seat next to them. Jump into the fray where you can by tossing out a brief comment, *"Wow, looks like everyone in Calgary has this flu!"* and see if they'll engage. If they're browsing through a magazine with a noticeable headline, you can comment on that or comment on their child, their outfit, a current event, or the old standby, remark on the weather, *"So, did you get caught in that deluge coming in today?"* If the person nearest you is trying to get through an article before their number comes up and their responses are terse, relax and let them be. Don't be such a nuisance that people start to move across the room from you. Be sensitive and courteous.

3. **Make it better:** Whenever you meet someone, ask yourself if there's a way that the *nectrified you* can improve that person's situation. I love to try to make people laugh and if I can find a way even in the briefest of instances, I'll do it. Don't use potty or put-down humour, just be your happy self. Life is full of opportunities for humour, especially if you're willing to laugh at yourself! Laughter is good for the body and soul and it's contagious.

4. **Ask Questions**: Memorize a couple of provocative little numbers to pop into a conversation when it stalls. Use questions that move people out of their stiff zone.

   - What's your favourite flavour of ice cream?
   - If you could spend an afternoon with an historical figure, who would you chose? What would you want to talk about?
   - Is there a movie in your collection that you've watched over and over? What do you like about it?
   - What's the most important lesson you've learned so far in your life?

The Nectar Effect

If you're in a business setting where you're required to be more formal, ask people how they got into their business in the first place and what they like best about it. Ask them to describe their ideal customer. Find out where they get most of their business from.

5. **Get Personal.** Don't refer to people as leads, prospects, followers or any other generic label. Get in the positive, affirming habit of using people's names. Instead of saying, I was chatting with a prospect yesterday, say I chatted with a mortgage broker named Cecil yesterday for example. Think of people as people, not as categories.

6. **Learn to listen.** If you catch yourself retrieving, forming and rehearsing your next comment while your conversation partner is speaking, stop it. Listen with your ears, your eyes, your body, and your heart. Take up the challenge to stay focused on your friend and even allow them to dominate the chat. Take note of this great story posted by Mark Phillips on his vertabase.com blog:

Gladstone

A women in England went on separate dates with two very famous people who had very different personalities, William Gladstone and Benjamin Disraeli.

Asked about her evening with Gladstone she said,

"*He took me to the symphony and by the end of the night I felt like I was with the most sophisticated and smartest man in the world.*"

And how about your evening with Disraeli? her friends asked.

"*He took me to the opera. By the end of the night I felt like I was the most sophisticated and smartest woman in the world.*"

Gladstone spent the evening talking about himself.

Disraeli spent his evening listening to her. Disraeli made her feel special. (read the post here: Gladstone.TheNectarEffect.com)

7. **Share information appropriately.** This is important at all times, but controlling yourself is critical when you're with someone and wish to avoid making them feel uncomfortable. Different people handle information differently. Some people like detail. Some people only want the abridged version. Some people process information quickly, while others must take time to reflect. Some take everything personally, others are open to correction. Read the person you're with by paying attention to their their eyes and body language. Work on this invaluable skill to enable you to adapt to the different individuals you encounter. It will help you quickly gauge your companion's enthusiasm or confusion.

8. **Act as if.** Pretend you're a confident, assertive person who knows how to attract people and how to make them feel valued. Describe in detail, using all your senses and every fibre of your imagination, what that looks like and how it feels and take time everyday to relax and envision the scenario you've just created. When you come upon an opportunity, act out what you've already practiced in your mind. I can tell you from personal experience that there are teeming numbers of trembling introverts out there trying to look and feel confident. If you believe that everyone you meet is one of those and put forward your passionate desire to help and encourage them, you'll forget all about your own shyness.

9. **Smile!** I came across someone on Twitter who claimed to be selling a health and energy elixir and in his twit pic it looked like his mouth was ready to slide off his face. It's critical to note that your smile is more significant than the sum total

of the rest of your appearance combined. If you're using all your Nectar to make extra-sparkling conversation this should happen naturally. In case your smile needs a warm up, practice your happy face in the mirror until it's as effortless to turn on as it is to don a decorative hat. If you feel silly, go with that by making a few silly faces and note how much more inviting your visage appears with joy splashed across it.

When you're with someone, focus on their face and eyes to where you're able to pinpoint their eye colour. Raise your eyebrows a touch to "open" your face but don't go pinching the bridge of your nose or scratching your receding hairline with them. Looking stern will scare people away. I regularly tell myself in my thoughts to relax my face and I'm often told I look ten years younger than I am. Try all of this. No one will be the slightest bit interested in mining your soul if your face looks rumpled and dejected.

10. **Create trust:** This sounds esoteric, but it's fairly easy to do, if, indeed, you are trustworthy. Don't blab to yourself about yourself as if the person you're with is a bystander. If you appear self-centred and you'll be left alone with yourself. Approach everyone with humility and consideration. Establish rapport by following some of the suggestions I've already made. Pretend you're a journalist wanting to get a the next big story. What kinds of questions do you need to ask to keep the person talking about themselves? Use questions that draw people out - *why do you think it happened like that? How did that make you feel? Hmm, that's very interesting - tell me more about that.*

11. **Learn to shake hands**. Don't offer someone a limp fish or crush their digits with your iron grip. No excessive pumping, you're not churning butter. A firm double shake and you're done.

Up Close and Personal

If you live in a city, you will constantly be presented with opportunities to relate to others as you go to work, run errands, take your exercise, etc. but if you're serious about making your business fly, you really need to create opportunities for connection over and above such chance occurrences.

1. **Volunteer in your community.** Your face and your name will become familiar and trusted.

2. **Take someone out to lunch every week.** Invite old friends and acquaintances to rekindle or deepen relationships; strangers and new business connections to build new relationships. Include past, present and future clients, as well as people who will never be a client - you never know who they know. You and your friends will benefit as you broaden your social circle and your influence. Make whomever you're with feel valued and appreciated. Send them a note of thanks for taking the time to be with you after the visit.

3. **Present workshops in your field of expertise.** Remember, don't sell, educate. Have a home business selling vitamins? Do a health and wellness seminar and don't talk about your vitamins, just present yourself as a person who's educated in health and wellness. Make sure you're well-versed on what you're legally allowed to present before you do this! If they want more information or help, you can point them to your products. If you're in the finance business, do a workshop on frugal living, on how to create a savings plan when you're are already maxed out or on how to pay off a debt quickly. If you're a landscaper, do a workshop on preparing your Winter soil for a Spring harvest. Share what you know without a hook and watch your business grow.

Now, this next part is important enough to warrant its own section!

Join a Networking Group

I believe in the efficacy of networking meetings as a way to gain new business and new business partners, but you need to know how to use them.

Don't go to a networking meeting to make a sale or gain a client on the first day. The chances are great that this won't happen. Referrals are made when people know, like, trust, and remember you. That doesn't happen in a 15-minute conversation except on a rare occasion.

These meetings are where you must unveil the Nectar. Do you have a handout that could help everyone in that room that doesn't blatantly sell your services? For example, if you're a real-estate agent you might put together a sheet on how to find new business that might be applicable to other businesses, too. Do you have a list of tools that help you to run your show smoothly and efficiently that you can share with others?

In your conversations, when people bring up issues they're struggling with, look beyond the frustration and endeavour to help them find a solution. Refer them to another business or online resource even if, especially if, it doesn't involve you. Whether they take your suggestion or not, make a note to check back and see if they were successful at straightening things out.

Keep the presentation of your own business brief, sweet and focused. Don't break out the marching band. State the fundamentals in one fun, relaxed sentence and let others take the floor.

Treat the meeting as if it were your own. Create the atmosphere you would like to have if you were in charge. Model good meeting manners by allowing people equal time to present, by listening thoughtfully and raising a hand to ask relevant questions and by not talking out of turn. Remember how much cachet a sincere compliment can give you. Hear something you like from a participant? Let them know at the close of the meeting what you appreciated and thank them for their input.

Commit yourself to riding the train to the final stop. Spend a full year in a networking group before you decide that it's not right for you, unless, of course, the group is truly offensive or clearly targets a market that will never be of benefit to you.

After every meeting take a moment to reflect on what new things you learned and how you will adapt and utilize them yourself. A vital key to a successful networking relationship is follow up. If you have success after taking someone's advice make sure you tell the story and thank the individual who proffered the tip publicly in the next meeting. If you were able to add your own twist to it, include that information as well. No one need be threatened by this, but all should applaud any innovation that occurs in the course of helping each other to succeed.

Which brings us to the topic of competition. Because we we live in a capitalistic economy, there will always be others vying for the same clients you are. I ran a chapter of a local networking group and right at the beginning a new person walked in whose 30 second elevator speech was pretty much the same as mine. I had a few options:

- I could show him the door
- I could create a permanent "one-upmanship"
- I could find a way to cooperate and even collaborate

I chose the third option. We sat down over coffee and chatted about our different backgrounds, philosophies and strategies. We discussed what we enjoyed and what made us cranky and near insane. In so doing, we discovered that each of us had different strengths and weaknesses and that if we worked together, sharing our positives, we could make both of our businesses better.

If you're confronted by your competition somewhere, I encourage you to do the same. Our unique giftings as individuals, when conveyed freely, enable us to create new, fresh ways of doing things. Your competition may be a whizz at prospecting and help you land new clients while you can teach them a thing or ten about follow-up and client nurture. When competing businesses work together, both parties are stronger for it.

If your competition doesn't want to play nice, spread nasty rumours about their abominable lack of attention to health and safety standards. Just kidding! I wanted to see if you were still with me. An integral part of the Nectar Effect is giving others the space to be who they are, and who they are not, without judgment. If someone rejects you, even squashes you, turn your petals to face the light and warmth. Someone out there is going to be into you and into the idea of creating a partnership for the mutual nourishment and growth of both your businesses. This kind of professional camaraderie will be seen as asset by those who are considering using your services.

Tips for getting started right away:

1. Invite someone to lunch. Challenge yourself to see how little you can talk about yourself while finding out as much as you can about the other person. And remember, if you do the inviting, you need to offer to buy the lunch for both of you!

2. Start researching a variety of networking clubs in your area. Schedule several over the next couple of months, and then zero in on one or two where you can not only benefit others the most, but where you'll find the best connections to your ideal client.

The Customer is Gold

I usually have between 23 and 27 adventures happening at any given time in my office. I might be working on a home school project for my kids, trying to make sense of the family finances and banking or tackling a personal interest research project. This is on top of a new product for my business, marketing tasks for my clients, goal setting activities and in my spare time I start or finish one of several books currently on my night stand. For a hobby I like opening and sorting sort the mail.

Each of these projects produces collateral document damage such as papers, book and magazines complete with the tools and supplies needed to create more damage. As a very visual learner I like to have all of it represented on my desk where I can see it or I'll forget about it.

In addition to this chaos, my desk becomes the depository for the miscellaneous fallout from the household universe such as objects that don't have an obvious home in the entirety of my house. For some reason they seem to gravitate to the tiny cramped confines of my desk. My office often looks like the cross between a "Where's Waldo" page puzzler and an episode of Hoarders Buried Alive. Try as I might, for some reason I couldn't seem to manage. Good thing I can work in chaos and have ready access to chocolate, tea, and more chocolate.

Whenever I entered this chaos I wondered if some portal would slam shut and I'd be lost forever, free floating in a swirling cosmic cluster of clutter. The Big Bang to me was more than a theory, it was taking over my office. Out of sheer panic I resorted to hiring professional organizers to rescue me from this cosmic debris field I still insisted was "manageable".

I met a pair of ladies at a trade show who did clutter busting. We were laughing together shortly after we met, which is a good sign that a relationship is forming, and I soon felt safe enough to admit I was organizationally challenged. They had immediate suggestions, so I hired them to help me. I wanted to take them home at the end of the trade show but felt it might look a little too desperate.

They were scheduled to arrive at my place on a Saturday after attending a local community fair. On their way, they messaged me and asked if I'd like a Tim Horton's coffee. A very small gesture, but a thoughtful one. It made an impression on me. They bustled in cheerful and encouraging, hot coffee steaming. They were proficient and fast and at the end of their visit I had an organized office that was still as such over a month later, even though I've taken on new projects. What I loved most about them was their thoughtful concern for me and their ability to make me laugh throughout what should have been a wretched load of suffering. When I talk about customer service, it can be this simple.

Zappos

Of course, customer service can and should knock your anklets off. Zappos, the highly innovative online shoe store (Zappos.TheNectarEffect.com), is a wonderful example of this. When Zappos hit that point in their business where they were forced to cut costs in order to survive, they decided they'd focus on offering unbelievable customer service to their existing clients instead of spending money they didn't have on marketing to acquire new ones. Their hope was that their current clients would be so delighted with what they experienced at Zappos that they'd tell their friends and spread the word. It worked.

My favourite story from Zappos is about a man who bought several pairs of shoes for his mother, because he didn't know what size she wore (I'm trying to get the details right - the original blog post has disappeared due to band width shortage!) Shortly after the shoes arrived his mother became ill. He became so involved in helping his mother that he forgot all about the shoes. The woman passed away and as this gentleman was cleaning out her things he came across the shoes. Knowing that he had now exceeded the time limit for returns, he called Zappos and explained the situation, asking if there was any way they could extend the return time. The shoes had never been worn.

Zappos said they were sorry for his loss and told him they'd send the UPS truck the next day to pick up the shoes, that there would be no charge for this and that he would receive a full refund. Not only did the truck arrive, but the driver had a bouquet of flowers and a card from the customer service person at Zappos expressing his condolences. Now, that's customer service! It might have cost the company a couple hundred dollars to complete this transaction, with no sale and a return at that, but they've had thousands of dollars worth of free, word-of-mouth advertising from this story that has probably resulted in hundreds of new sales. I'm not a big shoe addict, but I'm suddenly open to shopping at Zappos!

How many times have you dealt with a business only to feel like you were an interruption? How often do you have to nag a company for what they supposedly "specialize in"? Good customer service is all it takes these days to be noticed. Great customer service will make you unforgettable and, as it appears in the case of Zappos, profitable. They're swimming in Nectar and they're inviting people to join them.

How can we make this happen?

1. **Ask and Listen.** You need to start on the road to exceptional customer care by asking questions and listening. Ask your customers how they like your product, your service. Ask them what's missing. If they make a purchase find out why. If they didn't make a purchase find out why. Don't be intrusive, but explain that you need such information to improve your business and to enhance your customer service. Have an anonymous multiple choice client questionnaire ready that they can either fill out quickly at the counter or online when they get home. Take a look at what SurveyMonkey has to offer (Survey.TheNectarEffect.com) with regards to the online version. Also talk to people who *aren't* your clients about their consumer experience in general - your friends and family, online contacts, etc. Find out what their ideal would be in your industry. If some thing continues to come up, pay attention and take action.

    Survey

2. **Set your minimum.** Take a minute to decide what is your absolute minimum for customer service. Most franchise businesses have a sort of mantra that they have their employees memorize when dealing with customers, like this:

    - greet the customer with a smile,
    - listen carefully,
    - solve the problem cheerfully,
    - ask for the sale,
    - create an upsell,
    - complete the purchase,
    - thank the customer and invite them back.

The Customer is Gold

Create something like this as your baseline for customer service.

3. **Make it memorable.** Now that you have your basic plan in place, see how many notches that level of service can be raised. You want them to be so pleased and so surprised that they become mesmerized by it. You want them to be delightfully aghast. It doesn't have to be expensive. It can cost as little as a trip to Timmie's or Starbucks. Once you have the picture of what WOW service can look like, make sure it's communicated to all your team members. Dredge up every inspirational "Zappos-like" story you can find and start every staff meeting by having a different person read one aloud. Have a meeting to brainstorm ways you can make your customers feel important and taken care of. What you want here is to convert your customers to raving fans who are so crazy about you and your pampering that they can't help but tell all their friends about you.

4. **Empower your employees to do whatever is necessary to make the customer happy.** There will always be problems. Make sure your employees have the power to make it right. Tim Ferris, in his book *The 4-Hour Work Week* (4hww.TheNectarEffect.com) decided to enable his employees to make any decision necessary up to a cost of $400 to fix any customer issue. Over that amount the solution needed to be passed to him, but up to $400 was in the hands of the contact point. Determine a value you can afford and make sure this point is stressed in a meeting rather than lost in an email. You may be surprised at how creative and compassionate your employees are.

4 Hour Work Week

47

5. **Demonstrate what you expect.** In a family, a good parent will model appropriate behaviour for a child to imitate. You, as head of the company, must exemplify any skill you're asking your employees to develop. Here's the biggest key - you, as the manager, must treat your employees the way you want *them* to treat your customers. If you make your employees feel valued and appreciated, it will rub off on your customers.

6. **Reward your employees.** If your employees are delivering great customer service they should be rewarded, especially if they were able to regain the trust of an angry client. Make customer service results the basis for almost all rewards and bonuses. Relay to your staff the importance of sharing their successes to encourage and inspire others, to obtain feedback, and to talk about alternative ways of handling future difficulties. Time should be allotted for this in staff meetings and exceptional cases could even be written up in the newsletter. Recognize those who are excelling. Encourage and mentor those who are struggling.

7. **Create reminders.** Display visually powerful, colorful reminders about customer service near your computer, your phone, your front door and your sales desk. Make customer service the priority in every transaction. Did you know that gaining a new customer is 6 to 7 times more expensive than keeping a customer you already have? Businesses who were able to raise their customer retention rate by as little as 5% saw profit increases that ranged from 5% to as much as 95%.

8. **Keep customer service in the present.** We often think of the future, but you need to concentrate on always dealing with every client's present need and dealing with it in the best possible manner. If each interaction is a pleasant, positive one, the future will take care of itself, as you'll have earned the right to talk about new transactions. If you don't make

The Customer is Gold

your customers happy right now where they are, you will open the door of opportunity for your competition.

9. **Stop the gimmicks and build the trust**. You want to build a business by creating loyal, vocal, satisfied customers that you don't have to constantly try to connect to with glitter and gadgets. Each of the steps in your customer service strategy should build on the <u>know, like, trust</u> and *<u>remember</u>* concept.

Of course, these are all good ideas, but how do you actually apply them in a practical way to your business?

1. **Make yourself and your business visible**. Please develop a website, and preferably one that has been designed by someone who understands marketing. Don't just grab your great-uncles' 3rd cousin's nephew because he took a computer lab in High School. Make sure you have a mailing and/or street address in a place that's easy to find, along with a map for locals, a phone number, an email address, and a toll free number if your reach goes beyond your local area. Your website needs to be user and mobile friendly, all links working, with your hours of operation, contact information, FAQs and current specials available at the click of a mouse. You must be very easy to find when people are searching for you not only by name, but also by product and service. If you have an MLM/Network Marketing business, use more than your corporate page. Make your first connection through something like a blog or Facebook business page.

2. **Solve every problem as soon as possible.** When people are upset or frustrated over dealings with your company, reassure them that problems will be addressed immediately. Give your word that you will begin to work on the situation right now. If it's something that's going to take a while to resolve, make sure the client knows what your first step is and then keep them posted as you advance through to the resolution.

3. **Offer alternatives where the client is wrong.** If your client wants something that you know won't work or isn't possible, instead of telling them they're wrong, provide a list of alternatives and have them decide how they would like to proceed. There is almost always a way to find a compromise if you invest creatively in the conversation.

4. **Keep them informed**. Are you working on a long-term project? Put your plans for completion of the project in writing and frequently check in with your client with updates as to what you've accomplished. When giving your progress reports, provide feedback on the process, reasons for delays and any need for changes. Respond promptly to requests for clarification.

5. **Say thank you**. Often. For big reasons and small reasons. In many different ways - in discounts, gifts, cards, notes, emails, and in person. Share appreciation for your customer in each encounter.

6. **Apologize**. It doesn't matter who's right and who's wrong. Apologize if there's been a breach of trust or a misunderstanding. Even if you're right, apologize because you're sorry for the break. The only thing you'll gain by having to be right is the loss of a customer and a friend. Do whatever you can to remedy the situation. This is a wonderful opportunity for WOW customer service. Take full advantage of it.

7. **Never quibble over returns and always honour your guarantee**. A quick, painless return usually results in an increased sense of trust and a willingness to purchase again in the future - or at least the possibility your customer will share the story of how a problem was solved efficiently by your company.

    I used to work for a large department store, in their baby department. One day a gentleman came into the store pushing a well-worn, rather grubby stroller. In the stroller was an obese 5-year-old (I'm not kidding!) looking confined and uncomfortable.

The gentleman told me the stroller was defective. Under the metal footplate, the metal had been folded only once exposing a sharp edge rather than a smooth one. This was a heath concern for him and his child and he wanted his money back.

I examined the stroller myself in regards to his concern and, even though I have very small hands, there was no way I could access this metal edge. I couldn't see how any child could, either. The man was insistent that the stroller was poorly designed and his child was at risk.

I called the manager. She promptly agreed to accept a return on the stroller. Even though the model had long been discontinued, and it was obviously well-used in spite of the supposed defect, the gentleman received a refund for the current cost of new stroller.

It was obvious to me, a teenager at the time, that the stroller was by no means defective, but that this man was finished with the stroller and had the nerve to ask for a return rather than simply retiring it. I was shocked and appalled that my manager would so easily hand over the cash in this situation.

Now, however, I realize the value of that transaction.

8. **Answer all correspondence.** Whether online or offline, get back to your clients as quickly as possible. How quickly you can get back to your customer?

I hate housework. I especially hate dealing with floors. One year we bought my all-time favourite appliance: a Roomba® (Roomba.TheNectarEffect.com). Every afternoon at 3:00 pm it turns itself on, vacuums the whole main floor, then plugs itself back in to charge itself up for the next day's run. Meanwhile, I'm

The Nectar Effect

Roomba

Scooba

enjoying a peaceful afternoon undisturbed by thoughts of dust and grime on my floors. It is my new best friend. It makes me happy just walking past it in the morning on my shiny clean floor.

After about a month, it started making clicking noises. I sent their customer service an email and *in less than five minutes* I had a reply with a list of specific, easy to understand instructions that solved the problem. Was I impressed? You bet I was! Impressed enough that now I'm also looking at their floor-washing "Scooba®" so I not only don't have to vacuum, I won't have to wash floors either! (Scooba. TheNectarEffect.com)

9. **Design a rewards program for varying levels of engagement.** With the popularity of punch cards and point systems, people are looking for ways to maximize the value they get for their money. After gifting that first-time buyer, keep her coming back by making her aware of benefits of loyalty to your brand. Your staff should be well-versed in, and eager to share, this knowledge. Design a small card with your business Information, hours of operation and the key points of your loyalty program to remind your clients that it pays to come to you (if you're looking for a simple, inexpensive and highly profitable way to create a loyalty card program, contact me: Darlene@HotSpotSocialMedia.com).

Send Me an Email

Spoil good customers rotten. Shout out the long-term rewards of being a committed customer on your website e.g. birthday incentives and regular anniversary promotions only available to longtime clientele based on the number of years they've been with you. One-off surprises, like free shipping, tucking a little something into the package at no charge before sealing it up or dropping a special surprise in the shopping bag just before handing it over engenders loyalty and word of mouth advertising. Give some customer an unexpected, unadvertised discount. Be creative. Randomly. Create the element of delighted surprise.

10. **Treat your customers like individuals**. Be willing to bend the rules for your clients' special circumstances. Can you offer a customized solution to their problem? Of course, it's good to have policies in place and systems to follow to keep processes running smoothly, but recognize the uniqueness of every individual you encounter and be ready to improvise to keep them shopping with you. My Dad has a favourite expression when he's in need of something from a business that really shouldn't be that difficult: It's not 'can't', it's 'won't'. Never let a possible "won't" get in the way of customer service. If a request is doable and won't break laws or put you out of business, do it. It may be that these twists you perform to meet certain needs become a popular, regular offering for you and this is another instance where word of mouth marketing may come into play, as your client extols your flexibility and innovation.

11. **Work the adage *Under Promise and Over Deliver***. Make sure what you promise is great, and try to best that, as well. Look at every aspect of your business from reception to ease of ordering to shipping, etc. and aim for excellence at every juncture.

12. **Focus your efforts on the right people**. Ricky Nelson said, "You can't please everyone" and he was right. Not everyone

will be an ideal client. Find out who your service or product is best suited for and then shine for those customers. This is not about discrimination. You need to understand who you can best serve, and if someone is outside that circle, then the best thing you can do is to refer them to someone who is better suited to meet their needs. The ability to admit that you may not be a customer's best choice puts you in a positive light, makes your customer happier and provides someone else, who may return the favour, a new client. Contact the other business yourself, introduce your client to them and explain why you believe they're a better fit.

13. **Sort your priorities.** If your customer needs a wide range of services, make sure you prioritize their needs in the most efficient fashion so they get the best results in the shortest amount of time.

Tips for getting started right away:

1. Visit a dozen brick and mortar shops, call a dozen help lines and check out a dozen websites for customer service. Note what you like and don't like. If you like something figure out why and conceptualize how it might look in your business. If you don't like something, again, figure out why and work a solution so that it doesn't happen with you. Don't just stay within your own industry, but make your experimental field as wide as possible. My business is nothing like a shoe store, but I can learn from Zappos. If you can, involve your staff and/or team in doing their own research and bringing their findings back to you.

2. Have a meeting with your staff or team, share what you've learned and brainstorm ideas for making your own customer service WOW.

3. Prioritize what you've discovered and find one thing to apply as soon as possible to your business.

Pick Up the Phone

Marc Reece (MarcReece.net) was the new kid on the playing field in his company and was having trouble joining the team. He was coming in as the "hot shot", the guy who was going to show everyone how it was done. The sales team was less than enthusiastic.

Marc Reece

Wanting to gain their trust, he asked them to give him their list of tire kickers and no-buys. In his words, here is what happened:

> *My objective was to figure out why these people didn't buy when they were contacted and drum up some business. I called everybody on the list and followed it up with an email if I was not able to connect with the decision maker.*
>
> *After my introduction I asked the following question.*
>
> *"I understand that you did not do business with us in the past. Would you please tell me why?"*
>
> *60% of the answers I received were. "I did not do business with you because the sales person did not care about me or my business, they only cared about the sale. In fact it seemed the sales person did not want to learn about my business."*

The Nectar Effect

> *My response was always, "Thank you for taking time to share that with me. Would you mind telling me about your business and some of the current challenges that you are facing?"*
>
> *This experiment in relationship-based selling resulted in 30k dollars in revenue with an additional 45k in the sales pipeline. Sales are built on relationships and trust, doing what is in the best interest of the person buying the product or service rather than exclusively serving one's wallet.*

I really don't like to chat on the phone. I'm more visually oriented and I find it hard to spend long periods of time in conversation when I can't see the person I'm speaking with. Because of this, I tend to avoid the phone unless I'm using it to book an appointment or organize something that would be cumbersome via email or online chat. I can count on one hand who has my cell number. You'd think with my aversion to the telephone, I'd be all for an automated system. However, I can't say I know of anyone who likes the lady who plugs her nose and rattles off the levels of menu chaos one might get lost in. Farming out the first contact for your business may be necessary for large organizations, but it isn't a good idea for a small business. People who frequent small businesses are doing so for a reason, often because they like to support their local economy. They also like to know where the service or product is coming from on an organic level. Sometimes people just like to talk to a real person and choose to shun the coldness of the big conglomerations who tend to use automated systems.

Surprise your clients by answering the phone. Sounds crazy! Who answers the phone these days? You do, if you're smart. If you can't do it yourself, have a staff member with clear, friendly communication skills answer the phone to either direct their call or answer their questions. We're a small company, granted, but when the phone rings, I, the owner, founder, and president, answer the call. If I'm

Pick Up the Phone

not available when you call, I'll do whatever I can to call you back to be sure that everything was handled to your satisfaction.

The thing is, the phone is a wonderful way to quickly connect with a client. As a follow-up tool there probably isn't a better one on the planet, other than meeting with someone face-to-face. So many businesses drop the ball here, some even making the unforgivably huge mistake of not returning customers' calls when the customer is trying to hire them! I find it hard to get my head around that one. If a customer calls because they want to hire someone in your field, why wouldn't you call back?

Denise Addis, in an article she posted on Morristown.Patch.com, tells such a story. Denise wanted to replace her roof and called a number of companies in her local area, wanting to support local businesses, and ended up encountering the now customary "We're just too busy to talk to you" answering machine greeting. She left messages and waited. And waited. No one called her back. Her response to this is worth a read:

> ...maybe it is just me who is so susceptible to the power of the "phone call," but it is the "phone call" that will make me yours, forever. If one landscaper called me back and said, "I just can't squeeze you in," I would have remembered them. If one roofer had called me just to say, "I am so busy I won't get to you until June," I would have remembered them and I would have appreciated the phone call. My expectations over the years have been lowered substantially, to such a place where I am happy, very happy in fact, with just getting a "phone call." Some simple sort of acknowledgment that I came to you, seeking help that I am willing to pay for, and if you

Morristown Roof

could simply acknowledge me, even if you refuse me, just acknowledge me, I will be grateful. And I don't think I am alone in feeling this way. (Full story here: Roof.TheNectarEffect.com)

99 Percent

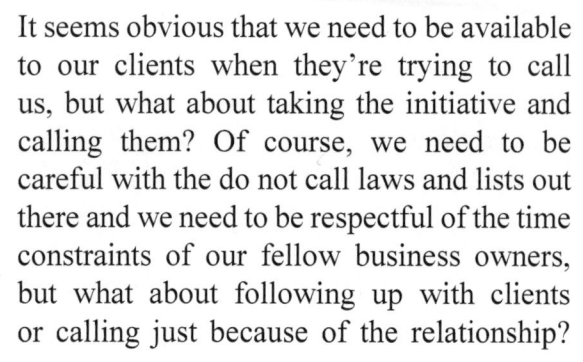

It seems obvious that we need to be available to our clients when they're trying to call us, but what about taking the initiative and calling them? Of course, we need to be careful with the do not call laws and lists out there and we need to be respectful of the time constraints of our fellow business owners, but what about following up with clients or calling just because of the relationship?

Christian Heritage Party

In 2009 the Christian Heritage Party in Canada was relatively unknown and decided to use a phone campaign with real people on the phone rather than an automated message to call the members of their electoral district to introduce themselves. One volunteer in Saskatchewan called a woman in Nova Scotia, introduced the party and their policies, and the woman in Nova Scotia became a true evangelist for the party, gaining them new votes and increasing awareness for the party. You can read that whole story here:Phone.TheNectarEffect.com

The story above is not likely to be repeated with the automated phone calls now going out around election time. As soon as I recognize it's an automated call from anyone, I hang up and I don't think I'm unusual in that way. If you interrupt me with a phone call, but I'm not important enough to speak to personally, I don't really care what you have to say.

Pick Up the Phone

Despite my telephone avoidance, I can't discount the power of a phone call over an email, social media status update, or even a card, to communicate my tone and intent.

In an article on his blog www.the99percent.com, Scott McDowell shares an interesting discovery. He says:

> *Earlier this year I attended a presentation with Daniel Goleman, author of Social Intelligence and godfather of the field of Emotional Intelligence . According to Goleman, there's a negativity bias to email – at the neural level. In other words, if an email's content is neutral, we assume the tone is negative. In face-to-face conversation, the subject matter and its emotional content is enhanced by tone of voice, facial expressions, and nonverbal cues. Not so with digital communication. Technology creates a vacuum that we humans fill with negative emotions by default, and digital emotions can escalate quickly... The barrage of email can certainly fan the flames. In an effort to be productive and succinct, our communication may be perceived as clipped, sarcastic, or rude. (Full story at 99.TheNectarEffect.com)*

For this reason, if you're going to share information that might be misinterpreted, use the phone. The phone allows us to hear the anticipation, the joy, the concern, or the distrust in our client's voice and allows them to hear the same in ours. Miscommunication is not as common over the phone as it might be in an email or online message.

The phone is also a great tool for positive reinforcement. To convey caring, it's second only to face-to-face communication and is a the next best way to establish a relationship where face-to-face isn't possible. On her blog "Newfangled" (NF.TheNectarEffect.com) Katie Jamison writes:

The Nectar Effect

New Fanaled

The best piece of advice I ever received about repairing a troubled relationship came from my brother, a man of few words who calls things like they are. As I analyzed and plotted my strategy to conquer the situation like a game of Risk, he stopped me cold in my tracks and said, "Katie, it's not that complicated. Just call them once a week." I had never considered that the solution to such a complicated problem could be that simple.

Client relationships aren't much different than personal ones in that they require routine, but substantial contact. And in most cases, email doesn't cut it. Never underestimate the power of picking up the phone to deliver news--even if it's something relatively insignificant that could be communicated easily by email. If you don't create space and time for a relationship to occur, then it won't. This rule isn't a complicated one, but there is no exception to it.

I have a dentist who personally calls me the day after I've had a major procedure done to see how I'm recovering. Her concern, expressed in a kind, timely manner, means a great deal to me.

University Connections

It is imperative that you sweeten your calls so that others will appreciate them. Many people may view your dial-ups as intrusions rather than welcome disruptions, but if you craft your calls with your client in mind, they can become as welcome as the call from an old friend. Jim Lavis, the Director and COO at University Connections

Pick Up the Phone

(UC.TheNectarEffect.com), shared his expertise at adding value to personal telemarketing:

> *I have been searching for the unique technique or that perfect approach to prospecting over the phone, but in my 25+ years in business the main conclusion I've drawn is that prospecting requires just plain old hard work and persistence. But this effort must be made in the context of certain preparatory steps.*
>
> *The first step involves doing your homework. For example, I often read blogs, articles, and trade magazines--just to mention a few--to learn what's important to my prospects. Additionally, I identify the prospects' needs by talking to relevant people inside and outside the organization (e.g., support staff, planning department personnel, suppliers, bankers, former employees, installers, etc.). In short, understanding the prospects' challenges and how those challenges relate to them personally will make a big difference.*
>
> *The next step is to contact the prospects in a way that shows you are already aware of their needs and you have specific solutions that have worked in the past. Accordingly, I often leave a message outlining a brief understanding of their dilemma, or I refer the prospects to a blog or web site link which describes what I have done for others facing similar challenges. This type of pro-active message greatly improves the odds for a return call and invitation to talk. Note that it may take multiple calls before the prospects realize that you have something of value to offer. And you do*

Sales Nurture

The Nectar Effect

need to consider what messages to leave and how to plan your calls on a case-by-case basis; the timing, frequency, content, etc. of the messages depend on what you've uncovered in the homework phase.

The Sales Blog

Overall, then, using these two steps will increase your chances of success by showing prospects that you respect their time by having already figured out what they probably need and that your solution warrants a review. The President and Chief Sales Officer for The Sales Blog SB.TheNectarEffect.com) has this to add:

Can you make them aware of changes that may impact their business? Can you inform them of industry trends that might be an advantage or a threat? Can you share with them a point of view that may help them better understand their own business or how they may achieve a greater outcome using a business like yours—even if it isn't your company they have chosen to use (yet!)?

...Instead of calling your dream client to check in and see if anything has changed, try this. Call and say: "We just identified a way to help one of our clients improve their profitability by 11%. Would you be interested in learning how we might be able to do the same thing for you? I am happy to share it with you." (for further information, see the whole article here: Nurture.TheNectarEffect.com)

Being prepared is the way to get your prospects attention, but you need to be clear, not only on what you're offering, but on your future plans for the relationship. Taking that satisfying step with a client from contact to contract is only the beginning.

Pick Up the Phone

Flyn Penoyer of TeleSales University (TSU.TheNetctarEffect.com) talks about making sure each call you make to a client moves them forward. He describes his efforts to land an account:

> *I called on a high tech company once and the first response I received was, "not interested." On my second attempt, the response was, "not now, too busy". On the third call, the answer was a much more hopeful, "this is something I'm going to need soon".*
>
> **TeleSales University**
>
> *Every time I spoke to them, I described what I do, making sure to add new biographical details in each subsequent phone call. At a particular point, I mentioned my experience with human resources and an appointment was set up for the next morning.*
>
> *At the end of our meeting together, I was intent on continuing to move forward in our relationship. After having helped him hire some salespeople, I asked if he had a CRM for the team. He replied that he had a purchase order on his desk he was preparing to sign. The short story is, he canned the PO and bought $7K of software and services from me.*

Now that we've discussed the advantages of picking up the phone, you may be asking, "When should I call?

1. **When something changes**. Has your offering changed? Has the industry changed? Has a particular situation affecting your client or yourself changed?

2. **When you discover something new**. Have you realized something you didn't know before that will help your client? Have you found a new product or system that would be of benefit to your client?

3. **When you need fresh input.** Are you working on developing a new product or service that might be of use to your client? Call and ask them for feedback on your proposal as to what they are missing at present or what they would find most helpful.

4. **When you need to keep the client "in-the-loop".** Are you working through a process that takes time, like an investment offering or a legal case? Instead of leaving your clients hanging, give them a regular two-minute update call, enabling them to keep tabs on your progress. This helps them to feel involved, assures them that you're watching out for them and that the case is proceeding on schedule.

5. **To go the extra mile.** Did someone purchase something from you? Call them up and find out how they like it. Ask them if they have an issue. Do they need a bigger size? A different model? An accessory to go with it? Do a search and call them back with the information. As memory serves, I've had only one company call me to confirm my satisfaction, which tells me that this kind of calling is an untapped opportunity for someone out there, especially a smaller company who isn't separated from their buyer by miles of middlemen. Do this and your customer's mild amazement will be a powerful motivator. When your clients start to mention you, the company who takes tender care of them, to their family and friends, people will be moving their accounts faster then you can say,"mass hysteria".

I'll wrap this up and show you how incredibly simple this is, by telling you what just happened. Talk about happy serendipity! I'm hyper-focused writing about the importance of a phone call and the phone rings. It's our dog's groomer. It's 9:10 in the morning and I was supposed to have the dog there by 9:00. For some reason, I hadn't yet shown sufficient love to my iPhone and I missed the reminder.

Pick Up the Phone

I don't otherwise miss appointments, but the dog groomers obviously aren't that special to me. I typically remember the appointment two weeks after it's passed and no one has ever called me from there before. Here are the problems with that:

1. We only book an appointment when my Bichon Shih Tzu starts bumping into walls or can no longer catch treats, because his hair's so long he can't see. If I miss an appointment at my busy groomer's, the poor thing is tripping over fur before I can get him booked in again. (Put the phone down, please. There's no need to contact PETA. Rest assured, in all other matters this dog is spoiled!)

2. My very busy groomer finds herself with holes in her day that could have been filled with paying customers.

But...because she took two minutes to pick up the phone and call, I jumped in the car and had the dog there in 10 minutes. She had a full day, I had a groomed dog and we both avoided the hassle of re-booking.

Tips for getting started right away:

1. Look through your list for a client who needs updated information on your offerings, or who might need an adjustment to the services you offer in order to get better results. Pick up the phone and give them a call.

2. Is there someone on your list who's under the weather? Are they undergoing some kind of treatment or getting some medical testing done? Have they recently experienced a loss? Call them to encourage them.

3. Is there anyone you can make a quick call to, reminding them of an upcoming appointment?

Schmoozing on Social Media

Joseph Ranseth (VineMultimedia.com) is a huge fan of the power of social media. Let him share his story:

The Social Media Adventure

Vine Multimedia

In 2009 I made a cross-country road trip from Phoenix, AZ to Toronto, ON. During the trip I was having a conversation with a friend about the value of social media relationships and in particular, the question of "are social media friendships, REAL relationships?"

I decided to do an experiment. I wanted to see just how authentic these connections were, so I posted my cell phone number to my twitter account and invited people to send me supportive messages when I got tired behind the wheel and my co-driver was sleeping. I was astounded by what happened. I received text messages of encouragement from around the world, literally. "Friends" from the USA, Canada, Mexico, Europe and even Asia were rallying to help me stay awake. I could feel the world uniting in making the roads a safer place! LOL

The Nectar Effect

I continued to post my cell phone # as we traveled (not having a smart phone at the time) asking for friends to text me with directions, recommendations on restaurants at certain cities, and even invitations to meet in person while I traveled along the way.

After meeting a handful of people, and seeing the significant impact these relationships were having, I decided to launch the Social Media Adventure, a cross-country road trip during the summer of 2009. (Adventure.TheNectarEffect.com) This adventure took me from city to city, meeting in-person, the friends that I had previously only connected with through social media. It was a live case-study in the power of social media to form genuine, authentic, in-person relationships. Seeing the unifying power of social media culminate in the physical meeting, whether it was at a tweet-up or one-on-one, I adopted the belief that the goal every social media relationship should eventually be a handshake or a hug.

Social Media Adventure

While there are still many of my friends & followers that I haven't met in person, the real value in being online is seeing many of those relationships grow into offline friendships or business relationships.

Even when I am not traveling, I continue to harness the power of the Social Media Adventure. Often I will play fun games with my followers by posting my cell phone number and offering a prize to the most creative text message, best movie suggestion, etc. The winners receive postcards, letters or other offline communication. The real prize, though, is always a deeper, stronger connection than when it was strictly just an online relationship.

Still now, I travel around and make a point to meet as many of my Social Media relationships in person. I detail these connections on my blog: Adventure.TheNectarEffect.com

Being a businessperson, I am often asked the question: Do I make money from my online presence? The answer is an emphatic yes, even though I do not directly promote the services of my marketing company through my personal social media presence. The approach of building authentic relationships based on common values & vision however has resulted in a significant amount of new business either directly with a friend that later evolved into a client, or by getting referrals from my online friends whose trust I have earned by putting a relationship as the focal point instead of just soliciting business.

I am passionate about social media. Having neglected what was once a highly developed skill of letter-writing, I have managed to lose contact with many dear friends from outside my immediate area or from other countries where I've lived, with no way of figuring out their current location. The arrival of Facebook has enabled me to reconnect with most of these people and I'm thrilled that I can contact them whenever from wherever and check in on a fairly regular basis without needing to find a working pen, a piece of decent, un-rumpled paper and a stamp, and not have to write a novella each time to make the contact worth the effort.

But beware! Social media is fun like a Mocha Coconut Frappuccino, a frothy pleasure but it can also be a perplexing pill because using social media as a tool to keep in touch and on top of things is one thing. Using it well to build your business is quite different, and abusing it will forever brand you a schnook. Being a schnook will sour your Nectar every time.

As with all forms of marketing, social media needs to be more about your client than you, but you still need to practice distributing your Nectar and you'll need to be skilled at it, as the Internet is an environment where we must use our imagination to fill in the gaps in our limited sensory perceptions. The term you want to focus on is engagement. It seems like there's a new platform or ultimate marketing strategy almost every day - don't panic over this. The key is to find the platform that your target market uses and spark your energy there.

Don't let anyone scam you out of your integrity with the promise of a gazillion followers. Followers ad nauseam will only end up making you nauseated, if their purpose is to spit out ticker tape links or plug up your timeline with incessant, banal chatter. You want people to follow you because they're intrigued by you, both as a person and as a business. It's not about the numbers, it's about meaningful connections.

With Facebook, you're going to be looking for people whom you know already: extended family, friends old and new, former classmates, co-workers, church members, etc. Whenever someone accepts your friend request, look through their list of friends. You'll be surprised at who they know and they may have been able to locate someone you were looking for. Be careful with mass connections, though. You can be reported and banned, if it appears as if you're requesting too many people you don't know.

With Twitter, you are free to request away, but there is a daily limit. It's seen as a courtesy to accept people's follower requests and It doesn't hurt you in the numbers department. Of course, you can create lists of individuals you wish to watch more closely in order to use your time on Twitter more effectively. Find your ideal client and, as was suggested above, sleuth friends from friends.

Schmoozing on Social Media

Your status updates/Tweets should be a mixture of personal and professional. Release the Nectar with funny anecdotes about your life, musings you've been wondering about, quotes you subscribe to, questions you ask yourself. You will avoid being labeled as a spammer if you reveal yourself and your business in a random, thoughtful, entertaining fashion. You may decide not to mention your business at all other than in your profile/bio and be pleasantly surprised at how much interest you still receive just through socializing. Regardless of the platforms you settle on, flesh out your profile with descriptive statements and pictures; as much information as you feel comfortable giving. Your picture/profile is about the Nectar and your unwillingness to share about yourself will put up a wall you'll have to scale with those who weren't afraid to be open.

There are many cool things you can do with social media, but you need to be aware of the differences between the platforms - how Twitter is different from Facebook is different from YouTube, is different from LinkedIn, etc. Spend time on any of the platforms and watch and read and observe before you jump in. Get a feel for how your target market - and your competition - are using these platforms and how they invite people to engage with them. Here's a fun guideline to using the different platforms effectively:

Twitter can be thought of as kind of an online cocktail party. Short, superficial conversations. The point of Twitter is to make the connection. It's a great place to research and connect with your target market, and get seen by them by commenting on and sharing what they post. It's also one of the best ways to stay on top of anything that's happening whether it's the latest political crises, or that abominable fashion faux pas. On Twitter you want to be posting inspiration, questions, and bits of information - both personal and business - that get shared so that you get your name out there. The ultimate goal is to move them from Twitter to a different platform where you can have a conversation, such as to Facebook or your blog. Because Twitter is so fast moving, you need to post between six and ten times throughout the day in order to be truly visible.

Facebook is the online Starbucks. Your conversations here can be lengthier, they can get a little more personal in some cases, and you can share more detailed information. Facebook also needs to be very visual. Not everything you share should be a picture, but you should have two to three posts per day that are visually stimulating. For example, if you're posting your blog to Facebook, make sure there is a picture on the blog post itself and then, instead of having it auto-posted to your Facebook page which just gives you a tiny thumbnail, post it manually, adding the picture in as a separate element so it really stands out. Facebook is more about conversation, so don't pound your followers over the head by posting dozens of times a day. Three to five posts done well, with a wide variety of subjects and points of interest, is usually plenty.

LinkedIn is a networking meeting. Don't talk about the new t-shirt you bought your min-pin, the details of your bistro lunch, or how much you loved the latest trashy novel. Business only. You can bring a personal touch to your profile, and occasionally post an off-topic question just for fun, but otherwise, don't waste time here posting small talk. The status update on LinkedIn is probably happy with two to four posts per week – just enough to keep your name popping up regularly. Don't forget to also participate in appropriate groups on LinkedIn for a real power-punch!

Pinterest is a scrap-booking party where folks get together to share hobbies and activities they like. If you're the kind to post dozens of pictures on Facebook, it would be better for you to switch to Pinterest as your platform. This is a great place to hang out if your target market is women, but it's great to see that more and more men and businesses are also getting involved in creative ways

Hootsuite

these days. On Pinterest you can post as many things as you like – this bothers no one. However, as with all platforms, consistency is the key. Don't post thirty pictures one day, and then disappear for a month. You won't build anything that way.

Google+ is more of a techie hangout that's full of early adopters and many industry thought leaders. One thing is for sure, Google loves it, and if you're there it will probably increase your page rank. My guess is that it might just sneak up and surprise us, replacing some of the platforms we currently know and love so well. Keep your eyes on this, and start becoming involved so you don't miss the boat.

Here are some fun ways to engage on social media platforms:

1. **Acknowledge birthdays.** Facebook will post most of your friends' birthdays. On Twitter, you can simply put "Happy Birthday" or "Happy Anniversary" in the search box and find those people you can celebrate. Do this even if you don't follow them. You never know what might come out of it. Don't spend a lot of time on this, but do a few just to spread your presence.

2. **Create a fun poll.** This is a way to give users a whiff of your Nectar. Make it silly, make it saucy, make it sentimental. When you get the answers in, turn the results into a blog post and share it with your friends. You can also do a serious poll about your business, but do honest research. Don't use it as a way to feign interest just to get a few clicks.

3. **Do a search for different hashtags.** Look for terms such as #question, #help, and/or your specific keywords and phrases to see if someone out there needs what you have. Don't sell, educate. Can you send them to a blog post that solves their problem? Is there a link you can pass along that leads to a resource or tool they might need? Do you know a person or business that can solve their problem, even if it's not yours?

See what you can do to help them out.

4. **Don't automatically cross-post everything from one platform to another.** These are different platforms and need to be treated as such. What works well on one platform doesn't always work on the other.

5. **Create a few videos for YouTube.** These don't have to be Hollywood quality. Grab your smart phone and film your team talking about what's important to them concerning your business and/or market. Put together a fun April Fool's stunt and share it on YouTube. You can also offer video courses by turning PowerPoint presentations into movies using Animoto (Animoto. TheNectarEffect.com). Use all the tools in your creative arsenal and have fun doing it. It's been proven that material presented in a medium that requires the use of multiple senses to access it is remembered better than just using words or pictures. Keep these short though, unless you're doing a whole course. A great length is three to five minutes.

Animoto

6. **Post your blog.** Use a program such as Hootsuite (Hoot. TheNectarEffect.com) to pop your blog into your feed several times a week. Update your own status on social media whenever you put up a new post, but make sure this is not the sum total of your presence. Take time to periodically go through your friends and family's updates and responding in your own characteristic way. Join one of the many groups on social media as well. You'll have the opportunity to share your story with others like yourself and promote your blog/ product/ service at the same time.

7. **Don't send the standard blueprint email to connect with people on social media.** Create your own, or add a personal

message to your invitation explaining why you want to connect, and what you see of value in the other person. The same goes for Direct Messages to those who follow you on Twitter. Don't ignore new followers. Check out their page, check out their website, find what you have in common and connect with a personal note that shares a common bond and a word of encouragement. If that person fits the description of your ideal client invite them to respond to a question, have them introduce themselves on your Facebook page, or find something else to move the relationship forward in a way that brings them a win. Please don't hammer them with links now that you're connected! As they respond, keep requesting bigger commitments that are still a win. Once they've interacted on social media a few times invite them to participate in a webinar you're giving, or download a free report you've created. Then lead them to join your mailing list, etc. It's important to be intentional, but it's also important to gain and keep their trust.

8. **Reward people for responding** when people engage with you on social media. Thank them if they've passed something along or complimented something you've shared.

9. **Take every opportunity to promote those that engage with you**. Try their services if you can and post praise where deserved. Share their information with people you know who can use what they have to offer.

10. **Find frequent opportunities to connect with your followers personally**. Do you have friends in complimentary industries? Connect them. Post a comment on their blog, answer a question. Whatever it takes to connect a little more personally will build a huge following of active, thoughtful fans for you and your business.

11. **Join groups on Facebook and LinkedIn** that reach your target market and allow you to share. When you have an

appropriate post that meets the needs of the actual group, not just the target market, air it. Don't spam or be a nuisance. Put out good content. Post thoughtful questions to stimulate feedback. Engage in conversation.

12. **Compile a list** of quotes that deal with your industry, along with questions, trivia, tips and a challenge or two. Ideally you want to start with a list of at least 200 items that you continue to update as you explore the Internet and read great books on your industry. Use this list to post four to five conversation starters on social media every day.

Bufferapp

Social Media in a Box

Once you have your list you can use something like BufferApp to automate the scheduling. (Buffer.TheNectarEffect.com)

If the idea of these lists feels overwhelming look at the Social Media in a Box program (SMB.TheNectarEffect.com)

13. **Share your product or service.** Intersperse this list above with your product specific posts (about one post in five should be promotional) but create these posts more in a conversational stye, rather than as ads that scream "Buy me! Buy me!"

Stumble Upon

14. **Everyone appreciates recognition.** Whenever you have a few minutes, for example when someone has put you on hold, when you're stuck in gridlock or when you're eating lunch with a cyber-

addicted friend who regularly disses you by preferring to talk to a voice on a wire over a present person, do a quick glance through your Twitter stream and re-tweet your followers. Responding to them is just as good. With Twitter, you don't have to worry about getting locked into a long conversation, as you only have 140 characters at your disposal and it's understood that people are in and out all the time. You can bow out and bow back in and it's not seen as rude in the slightest. On Facebook, you can do a quick in and out by liking people's status updates and everyone likes to be liked, don't they?

15. **Tag the appropriate people** where possible, to increase their engagement, but please don't post a photo and tag all your friends just so they'll take a look. Tag only the people IN the photo.

16. **Has someone achieved something?** Are they celebrating something? Are they frustrated or angry? Respond. Be specific so they know what you're referring to. Do your best to encourage and support people, because you care.

17. **Do a search for your actual name, your business, or your product/service** and see if anyone's talking about you that you might have otherwise missed. Graciously respond to what they wrote with the intent of drawing them into a conversation.

18. **Be interesting.** Share tidbits that you discover in your travels on the net. Maybe you have a family member who has a penchant for quirky trivia. Use services like StumbleUpon to find unusual things to share - again, not always about your business, but always stimulating. (Stumble.TheNectarEffect.com)   You can sit down one afternoon once you've located several of these kinds of posts and sprinkle them throughout the list you created in step 12 with the quotes, questions and tips.

The Nectar Effect

19. **Ask questions for elaboration and clarification.** Asking questions helps solidify the information in your mind and helps the person sharing focus her thoughts and intentions. It's good for both of you and it keeps the conversation going.

20. **Laugh at yourself.** Show your followers you have a sense of humour by mentioning status updates or quotes that made you smile or giggle. Demonstrating your ability to loosen up and be silly is a sure way of spritzing your Nectar. Share your own bloopers as long as it won't offend others. Try keeping it sassy, but classy. Commiserate with others over their mishaps, if they're sharing them in a humorous fashion. Ask an either/or question: *Would you rather be creative or organized?* and offer your own goofy response to heighten the fun. Challenge yourself everyday to come up with something so provocative that your number of responses continues to increase.

21. **Give people a shout out.** Go through your list of followers and find someone who's working hard and give them a boost on Facebook and Twitter: *Hey, check out my friend @ username! If you need plumbing in Ottawa, he's your guy!*

22. **Keep it concise, keep it comprehensible, keep it sweet.** Craft your status updates carefully. Proof them before hitting send and reread afterward. Social media forums are great taskmasters when it comes to requiring us to get to the point. You have the equivalent of a crawl space to express yourself in. Use *2, 4, B, C, R, U*, anything that you can substitute for a word that will give you more square footage to include the truly great content. Do your best to create something that your followers will view as a worthwhile interruption to their day. Think about those followers you've blocked in the past, the food diary friends, the people of the four letter words, the peeps with the obscene twit pics, *the I live to whine* club, the *my life is better than yours will ever be* linkers. Hopefully, it's easy for you not to be like these.

Schmoozing on Social Media

Now, think about those followers that you're drawn to that you wish you knew better. They're effective at distributing their Nectar. Analyze their updates to see what you can learn from their success. If you don't feel confident regarding your writing skills, there are countless users who pass on the quotes of others. Pick a theme: humorous, motivational, target specific, etc., find an bookmark a quotes site and start collecting, organizing and dealing them out. In case you do wish to tone up your writing chops, have a trusted friend, one who you know is a good communicator, read some of your posts and give you their honest feedback. Putting things in your own words is a Nectar-positive choice. Expressing your personality in this way will help your followers get to know you and trust you sooner.

1. **Be personal.** Remember that social media is a tool for building relationships and these relationships are what feed your bottom line. Give your followers a glimpse of who you are. Share a little about your hobbies, your likes and dislikes, your lifestyle and values, etc. Be open and inviting and don't be afraid to be vulnerable, but also be sensitive and show some restraint. Don't go psycho and rage about your ex-wife's newest boyfriend or share "Shock photos" of your pet political rant. Your junk is just that. The Internet is not the place to take out the trash. Think carefully about the impression you want to make and watch also that you don't become too negative or reveal things that could get you into trouble with others.

2. **Post photos**. Put up those pictures that show you in everyday life enjoying your family, your hobbies, your adventures in travel and relaxation. Avoid those pics that reveal a serious lack of judgment on your part; any drunken activity that would make you look like an adult stuck in adolescence, that candid shot your wife caught of you rolling your eyes at the mother-in-law. (I'm just kidding. None of us really have

any of those pictures, do we?) The key is to find photos that show you at your best; pictures that put you in a positive light, having good clean fun. If someone else has posted a compromising picture of you, simply "un-tag" yourself so it doesn't show up on your friends' streams.

3. **Start a mystery photo game.** Share a photo of a person or a place and have people guess who or where it is. Use a photo editing site to modify the picture to make it more difficult. Give a prize, such as a discount coupon or free consult, to the first one to guess the right answer.

4. **Use a unique hashtag** to share the first part of a riddle and let people guess the answer. Use Storify (Storify.TheNectarEffect.com) to collect and display the answers at the end of the day.

Storify

5. **Use your social media channels to ask your followers for input on a specific blog post topic** and share the resulting blog with everyone when it's done. This will make your followers feel like you're genuinely interested in their ideas and opinions. Be the first to comment on their submissions and use questions to encourage the formation of a dialogue.

6. **Use geo-targeting to find local social media connections** and hold a Tweet-Up to meet these people face to face. Nectar is so much easier to transfer in an offline social setting. Keep it public, open with some fun ice-breaker exercises, give everyone a chance to introduce and plug themselves and their business, and leave ample time to visit. Food and drink relaxes people. See if you can convince some local businesses on Twitter to sponsor the event.

Schmoozing on Social Media

7. **If you're going to be tweeting rigorously** about a particular event or news item or sharing conference updates that are important for only a small percentage of your clients, that may annoy the rest of your followers, give them a heads up ahead of time, and suggest they use a service like Proxlet (Proxlet.TheNectarEffect.com) to tune it out.

   Proxlet

8. **Give away valuable information** to your followers, an e-book, a course, a webinar, etc. Everyone likes to get freebies and your extra-value gifts may be the carrot they need to become a client.

9. **Thank those people individually on Twitter or Facebook for sharing your content**, highlighting your business or for any other favour they've performed. Public thanks puts your prospects and clients in a good light and encourages them to do the same for you and others.

10. **Contribute to what's already happening.** Is there a topic of the day? A big news item? Check the side of your Twitter page to see the current hot topics and join in the conversation. Show yourself to be a well-rounded, intelligent individual who has more than marketing and sales on her mind. Get your Nectar talking. Take every opportunity to positively convey who you are in all your uniqueness.

11. **Keep your tweets to under 120 characters** so they can be re-Tweeted. Re-Tweet others generously and you will gain more followers and the ones you have will become even more loyal.

Social media can become addictive, even more so when you convince yourself that hunching over your computer clicking for hours is for the betterment of your business. Bear in mind that your actual business must still be managed. In the case of social media, three scheduled 15-minute time slots at different times of the day will give you plenty of opportunity to connect. Checking in throughout the day will ensure you connect with more of your followers. See how many new people you can touch everyday.

Tips for getting started right away:

1. If you don't already participate in social media start asking your clients where they hang out online. Join the platform mentioned most often.

2. If you're on social media but feel overwhelmed and confused about how to get it up and running effectively take a look at the Social Media in a Box website (SMB.TheNectarEffect.com) and see if you can find the help you're looking for.

Social Media in a Box

3. If you already participate in social media somewhere let me encourage you to find some new people to follow and observe. Watch what others are doing and see what you can learn from them.

The Magic of a Greeting Card

I had the privilege of spending a few years in France – in fact both my children were born there. We lived on a beautiful acreage in the foothills of the Alps and our house looked out onto forever from each window.

We loved it there, but I was pretty isolated with two small kids and no car. My day had 2 highlights: my husband coming home and the arrival of the daily mail.

I'm not sure what it is about the mail, but there's something magical about knowing someone thought of you and put pen to paper. Don't we all dig through the ads and the bills with that tiny window of hope that someone, somewhere, thought of us?

While I love mail from friends and family, I never thought about using the power of a personal card in my business until one fateful day...

Because I've worked so hard to be visible online my contact information is everywhere, and it often gets appropriated for marketing purposes by people in the network marketing industry. Now I have nothing against network marketing – in fact I love the industry - but the sales tactics are often a little on the smarmy side. Over the years I've received countless invitations so join various companies. One company's reps in particular seemed to find me over and over – Send Out Cards. It was always the same story. In my pile of mail I'd see something that looked like a real card. I'd open it, curious, only to find it was just a solicitation. It simply got tossed in the bin without a second glance. Honestly, I just didn't have the time for another business, and really, no one wants a cold solicitation without any kind of real connection.

Recently, however, a new acquaintance approached me about this same business. I listened politely, and gave her the answer I gave everyone. I need to focus on what I'm currently doing. My friend was understanding, and we enjoyed the rest of our visit.

I received a card from her in the mail. It had a photo on the front cover of a hand holding *my* business card. Inside was a short note thanking me for spending time with her and listening to her proposal. She also touched on topics we'd discussed outside of business and offered a couple of very helpful ideas.

The card was written in her handwriting and signed with her signature. I was impressed, to put it mildly. The impact of this gesture caused me to not only sign up as a rep so I could use it, but it created a huge shift in how I conducted my business from then on. I went from *just like the other guys* kind of marketing to making my clients feel like the unique individuals they are. I'm just now seeing the results, but one thing I can tell you is, when I call a new prospect after having sent a card, they always know who I am, they always reference the card, and they're always willing to listen to what I have to say.

A survey from the American Greeting Card Association stated, "giving a greeting card creates a lasting impression and emotional bond between sender and receiver". In a national survey for the Greeting Card Association, nearly one-third of respondents said they keep the special cards they receive forever. Wouldn't you like to have that kind of connection with your client?

The power of a personal, thoughtful card can't be overestimated. Here are just a few examples of their influence beginning with my co-author Polly's own experience:

The Magic of a Greeting Card

Growing up, I received a birthday card every year from my parents as, hopefully, we all do. It wasn't the poetry or the artwork that caused me to save and reread these cards over the years. It was what was written on the back or the inside cover; a handwritten list by my Dad of all the things he liked about me. Whenever I'm feeling down, I get out those cards and have a visual reminder of not only how much I'm loved, but how much I've grown.

Few businesses, however, realize the power of the greeting card. Aliza Earnshaw, previous Director of Sales and Marketing and former Editor in Chief of AboutUs (About.TheNectarEffect.com) shared this story with me:

About Us

I work at an Internet company that spends a lot of time and effort cultivating real relationships with real people. So much of our presence is cyber that I'd almost forgotten about the impact of old-fashioned snail mail, until a local business owner reminded me.

I bought a pair of earrings from a jeweller who's in my office building, Grayling Jewelry. The owner, Katy Kippen, was delightful and friendly, and I enjoyed the experience of being in her shop. (Grayling.TheNectarEffect.com)

Grayling Jewelers

But I was really bowled over to get a handwritten thank-you card from her about 10 days or two weeks after buying the earrings. It came in the mail, to my home address, and it was a tasteful, sweet card that clearly

> *showed she knew exactly who I was. It wasn't an automated mailing - it was exactly like getting a card from a friend.*
>
> *Of course, that's kept Katy and her work in my mind. I'm thinking about buying a piece of her jewelry for my daughter, and now I'm wondering if I dare indulge in another piece for myself. I'll probably get both!*

There's something deeply satisfying about getting a colourful envelope in the mail that is neither a bill nor an ad. How many pieces of mail like that have you received this week? When the information in the card is handwritten, creative and meaningful, in that it refers to the client instead of your business, the effect is immediate and long-lasting.

Here's how I use them as a follow up tool:

1. Whenever I meet with someone for the first time, business or otherwise, I obtain their contact information and send a "nice to meet you" card. If it's a business connection, I put a picture of their business card on the front, using the same card template my friend used. If a personal contact, I try to put a picture of the recipient, which I've pulled directly from the Internet, on the front of the card set in a frame. I write succinctly noting those aspects of our meeting that I learned from and appreciated and close by thanking them for meeting with me. This is a computer-based program, but it's not an automated stock card. The card system uses my own handwriting and I sign it with my own signature. I then put a small picture of myself along with my name and my website URL at the bottom of the card, but otherwise there's no mention of my business, and no soliciting whatsoever.

2. I make a note in my Send Out Cards contact management system to call in two weeks – which is a week after the first card arrives - to set up a second meeting. By this time,

The Magic of a Greeting Card

Mackay 66

I've researched the person online using the Mackay66 as a guide (66.TheNectarEffect.com) and I've prepared notes for myself about their background and the things we might have in common. I also look up their online presence to build value into our next meeting. I do so to see if there are specific suggestions I can give that they can easily accomplish themselves (as I'm a social media coach/trainer). If they need something that I can do quickly to improve their visibility and reach, like uploading their existing graphic to their Facebook page, I offer to do that for free.

3. After this stage I know whether an ongoing conversation is likely - either because we connect well as friends, we see each other regularly in some sort of an interest group setting like a networking meeting, or this person has confirmed that we'll be doing business together - and if so, I let the relationship evolve, but I write myself reminders to check in regularly, usually by phone.

4. If it's unlikely that we'll see each other much, I'll put them into a physical card campaign that I personalize especially for them. In this campaign, the cards show up every month comprised of ideas to improve their business, such as a series of cards that share fun marketing tips or great ways to follow up, etc. At about the third card, I might send them a $10.00 Starbucks card and make the suggestion that self-employed people rarely have time to kick back and relax. I invite them to take a break with my compliments.

5. After about 6 months of useful information, I send them a card that has four of my business cards attached. I ask if they know of anyone who may be in need of my services and if they would mind passing my name along if, by chance,

The Nectar Effect

they came across such a person. This is the first time I ever mention my company in any way other than the small URL at the bottom of the card.

6. After the campaign is completed, or interrupted, as I mention below, I move the person to a quarterly campaign and send them a fun card celebrating an "odd" holiday - like Blue Popsicle day, or Ferris Wheel Day. My business information is not in these cards at all, just my name, but after six months of getting cards this is not necessary as they know who I am.

7. If at any time in the card series we connect on a professional or friendship level, I simply stop the campaign and continue the relationship with the appropriate responses.

8. If someone signs up as a client, I also send them a card to say thank you along with a small gift. I like to send brownies and who doesn't like these or at least know someone who does? I then follow up with cards every two months that introduce the team and our services.

Jackie Ulmer

Celebrate!

I am constantly tweaking and testing different follow-up processes with these cards to get the best results.

Follow up isn't the only way to use cards, but it beautifully augments any other medium you've been using to keep in touch with your clients and prospects.

Here are some other great ideas:

Creative Cards

The Magic of a Greeting Card

1. **Send a birthday or anniversary card.** If you're on Facebook and your friends have put their birth dates in their profiles, you can access the calendar to help you keep track of these important dates. Go to your home page, not your profile page, and on the left hand side under your picture click *events* then look down at the bottom of that page and click *birthdays*.

   31 Days to Greeting Card Mastery

2. If you can't find the birth date or anniversary of a client or prospect, send them an unbirthday or unanniversary card. I tend to send the unbirthday card about 3 months into the relationship and the unanniversary card about 4 months after that. Bruce Brown the author of "31 Days To Greeting Card Marketing Mastery" a great little book (31.TheNectarEffect.com), suggests writing something along the lines of, *"I'm not sure if your birthday is coming up soon or not. If I'm close, great! Happy Birthday. If not, and you feel comfortable doing so, please send me your birthdate and I'll be sure this is on time next year"*. If possible, I have a picture of the receiver beaming on the front of the card. Feel free to put in a gift certificate for your services, but don't send the card with your business card or a discount coupon, unless you're going for insincere. Don't wish someone a Happy Birthday and snatch it back with a "tell your friends about us". Their Birthday is not about you. Celebrate them or don't waste the paper.

For those of you who are skeptical of the benefits of sending a card, The Customer Connection (Custcon.TheNectarEffect.com) conducted a survey for a client/restaurant as part of the establishment's regular practice of mailing out birthday cards. They measured the response of 7,000 members of the restaurants loyalty diner program who had not visited the restaurant for over six months prior to receipt of the birthday card. When they analyzed this, they found:

Customer Connection

- 1,600 of the members who received a birthday card visited the client's restaurants during their birth month:
- 880 members redeemed their birthday card
- 720 members dined in the restaurant but did not use their birthday card
- In addition the 7,000 recipients of the birthday card dined 1,750 times in the restaurant during the 5 months following their birth month.
- The 7,000 members who had not visited the client's restaurants for over six months prior to receipt of the birthday card made a total of 3,350 visits to their restaurants during their birth month and the 5 months after.
- The client realized incremental sales of $100,000 at a cost of $7,900 for printing and mailing the birthday cards.

3. **Celebrate a fun day**. As I mentioned above, send a card for a fun holiday. There are several lists of holidays you can use. I like *Special Days to Celebrate* (Celebrate.TheNectarEffect.com). It's for families of small children, but there are often interesting links, recipes, and activities that you can also include in your cards.

4. **Send a note of congratulations** for engagements, weddings, births, graduations, promotions, new business, condolences, etc. Be outrageous! Send a card for no other reason than you were thinking of that person. Your business presence in these cards should be very small, if included at all. Except under

special circumstances, these kinds of cards should be people to people, not business to people and if you've been doing a good job of follow up, they'll know who you are without the accompanying plug.

5. **Send a note with a link to an article or event** that might be of interest to your client. Use a service like an RSS Reader (RSS.TheNectarEffect.com) to search the web for these items and send them to your in-box automatically. Scan this list every week and take a few minutes to forward appropriate material to enhance your client's lives and businesses.

6. **Has your client moved?** Send them a housewarming card with a small gift. If possible, put a picture of their new house on the front of the card

7. **Send a note of apology when you've messed up**. We all make mistakes. Own up without making excuses. Make amends by not only rectifying the error, but going beyond that. Offer them a movie pass for two or enclose a gift card for a nice dinner at a local restaurant. This over and above appeasement may just erase the mistake from their minds and restore the relationship.

8. **Celebrate your client's success**. Jackie Ulmer, a business coach, (JU.TheNectarEffect.com) offers a brilliant suggestion of having personal trainers take monthly pictures of their clients' improvement to send out with cards containing motivational messages (she has even more creative card marketing ideas here: Cards.TheNectarEffect.com). Share your area of expertise and keep your clients focused on their goals, not on yourself or your business. For example, if you're in real estate, you could send tips on improving resale value. If you're a landscaper, you could share the different tasks that need to be completed in a timely fashion in each season. If you're a restaurant owner, you could share ways

The Nectar Effect

to streamline food prep and promote some of your popular recipes. In all of these instances, help your target market by keeping your profile low while providing maximum value. Keep these cards informative and fun and your clients will love you for it.

9. **Send a referral.** Did you come across someone who could use the services of another business you know? Connect your clients. Send a card to each party that includes the appropriate contact information and follow up with a phone call. Make business for other businesses without expecting return. What goes around is bound to come back your way!

10. **You can also prospect with cards.** You could send a personalized teaser postcard to specific people in your target market. Depending on what you're offering, you could say something to the effect of, "What if I could show you how to improve your current real estate business by 32% for very little cost or time investment?" On the back of the card you could write, "Hi, John! I've noticed how proactive you are in marketing your real estate business with your entertaining newsletter. Knowing the value you place on "out of the box" thinking, I believe I have something you might be interested in. Call me if you want to chat: 403-555-1234". Mentioning their service or product and their efforts to market it shows that you're watching them and may keep your note out of the recycling bin.

11. **Send thank you cards.** Sending a thank you card is a great way to begin the day both for you and for your recipient. In his book *A Simple Act of Gratitude: The Year a Simple Act of Daily Gratitude Changed My Life* (365.TheNectarEffect.com) Lawyer

A Simple Act of Gratitude

The Magic of a Greeting Card

John Kralik found that by mailing out a hand-written thank you card every day, he was able to turn his failing business around and bring healing to his family and friendships. Through this process, he ended up sending several notes to an attorney who had sent him business on a number of different occasions. The attorney remarked that the notes kept John top of mind and aware that the referrals were appreciated. He mentioned that, in their absence, the attorney would have wondered if John already had all the good cases that he wanted. That's powerful.

Tom Hopkins used to write ten thank you notes every day and his business was soon being built almost exclusively by referrals. The same with Joe Girard, the most successful salesman ever, according to the Guinesss Book of Records. His trick was to send every client 13 cards a year - one every month just to say "I like you" and one for the holidays. He ended up hiring staff whose sole purpose was to write these cards, as he ended up sending 9000 cards every month, averaging 400-500 cards a day. People lined up to buy from him, often needing to book an appointment in advance. Did this work? Judge for yourself:

- Joe Girard averaged about 6 retail sales per day.
- From 1963 to 1977, he sold more cars one-on-one than anyone else *in the world*.
- Once he sold 18 automobiles in one single day.
- In his best month he made 174 sales.
- In his best year he sold a total of 1425 vehicles.

Need some ideas as to when to send a thank you card? Take your pick:

- **A prospect accepts your call** – We're all busy. Most people hate talking to sales people, so if you get through to someone and they don't call you a bleeping, bleepity bleeper and slam the phone down, send a thank you card.

- **You meet with a prospect** – Time is our most precious commodity. Thank those who are willing to get face-to-face in this world of texts and emails.

- **When someone purchases your product or service** – How often do you have someone contact you after a purchase is made to thank you again for choosing them and to inquire as to your continued satisfaction? Keep yourself at the front of your clients' minds by appreciating them when they sign on the dotted line, but don't stop there.

- **When they choose NOT to buy your product or service** – They took the time to come and investigate. Just because they didn't buy, doesn't mean they won't in the future. Thank them for their time and consideration.

- **After an event or presentation** – Send one to both the presenter and the organizer including pictures of the event.

- **Whenever you receive a gift** – I'm actually hoping this one is blatantly obvious

- **To acknowledge someone's faithful service** – Send one to that chipper personal assistant, the efficient and friendly postal clerk, the printer who is always gracious about doing the rush job on your business cards and doing it right.

- **On client anniversaries** – Steadfast love deserves to be acknowledged and loyal customers deserve to be rewarded. If they've been a client for one month, six months, one year, five years, send them a card. I become annoyed at companies who give gifts to first time customers and ignore their longtime clients who are the true building blocks of their industry. Ignore these supporters at your own peril as the price will be a crumbling foundation no longer able to prop up your generosity to strangers, nor the lifestyle you've grown accustomed to.

The Magic of a Greeting Card

- **Thank your employees and partners** – You can't hope to produce a quality product in a caustic environment where your employees and your service providers feel used, abused and neglected. Too many disgruntled employees booted out or running for the automatic doors will ruin your reputation with consumers and the business community alike. Be the company employees are clamoring to be a part of because of your ongoing commitment to helping, encouraging and appreciating your staff.

If you're now considering using cards, don't try to backtrack through 15,000 people in your contact files. Use them with your new clients to follow up and see what happens. This will enable you to better measure the results of your new strategy. If you find it's working for you, you may want to hire someone to begin adding past clients to your card system and build their use up in a more relaxed fashion over time.

Tips for getting started right away:

1. Purchase 20 note cards and 20 stamps.
2. Start at home plate. Each day send a card to a different staff member until all have been duly thanked. Note their unique contributions and praise them for their creativity, competency and efficiency. Watch for the effects of your work in employee morale, productivity and innovation.
2. If you have cards left over, send these to your most valued clients.
2. Don't forget to note people's responses. This will help you tweak your new marketing technique to ensure it hits the target in the heart and wallet every time.
2. If you want to take a look at Send Out Cards here's a link: SOC.TheNectarEffect.com. You can even send a free card if

The Nectar Effect

you like and test it out. If you sign up as a distributor I'll send you my follow up card campaigns so you can use them as a model for your own.

A Little Gift to Remember Me By

When I signed up for Send Out Cards I was already good friends with my upline and assumed things would move forward they way they always did in my previous network marketing history. I would basically be ignored unless I initiated the contact.

Wrong.

About 1 week after I signed up, my kids and I, along with my co-author Polly, were working hard in my house trying to re-purpose our basement into a useable home gym as a surprise for my husband's 50th birthday. We'd spent the morning sweating, getting all the junk down there sorted out, tossed, re-organized, boxed and cleaned. After about 4 hours we were feeling pretty ragged. We came upstairs for a break and I sent my daughter and the dog to the mailbox (highlight of my dog's day!) My daughter came back with an unexpected gift box from Send Out Cards. In the box was a lovely card from my upline thanking me for joining her in this business, as well as four cellophane-wrapped brownies that I did not share, no way, no how! Kidding, kidding. I did share them. I was delighted that there was one for each of us!

Again, I was struck by the power of such a simple idea. The brownies were a delightful, unexpected treat after having worked so hard all morning and Send Out Cards was permanently and positively branded in my brain. I stole this great idea and I now use it in my own business. New clients now receive a thank you note and a box of brownies.

Gifts, samples and SWAG (**S**ouvenirs, **W**earables, **A**nd **G**ifts) are just another powerful way to build your business, if used wisely and well. A company must exercise discernment in knowing which such sundries will create a return, but used effectively, they can be a real boon for your small business.

The truth is, clients are more willing to share referrals when there are goodies involved. This was tested with 20 Mary Kay consultants. Half of the consultants gave small imprinted lint removers to clients and half gave nothing. All of the clients were asked to share names of acquaintances who might be willing to hear about Mary Kay products. Here are the results:

- The willingness to share a referral was 14% higher in customers who received a gift.
- The sales people offering the gifts received 22% more referrals than those who gave no gift.

Think about your client and what their preferences and needs are. Think practically, but also think elegance or frivolity or fun. How can you make a lasting impression on your clients and connections so they remember you the next time they need your services or product?

Before you spend any money, ask yourself a few questions:

1. **Who is the recipient of the gift?** You can give a business person a sparkly purple rubber gummy hand and he may politely chuckle a little, but you can be fairly sure it's going to end up between the seats of the SUV covered in lint and hair. On the other hand, a small, stylish notebook, or a small cleaning cloth that sticks to the back of her cell phone might well be something a person might carry with them all the time. Know your client and their tastes.

A Little Gift to Remember Me By

2. **What are you wanting to achieve with your gift?** Is it for remaining "top of mind" with your client? Is it sharing the message or theme of your business eg. healthy living? Is it emphasizing your values eg. being trustworthy, simplifying lives, efficiency, etc. Or is it educating your audience with tips and strategies?

3. **What is your budget?** If your swag is expensive, test it in very small quantities and obtain feedback from your clients before you go gaga and blow the cash on a stash that's not going to help you achieve your goal.

4. **Is there a qualification** for receiving swag or are you willing to give it to anyone? Do you have criteria set up in your rewards program for sending a gift?

5. **Does the gift you've chosen support your marketing message?** In other words, are you giving out artsy ashtrays at a health and wellness conference? I believe in the power of symbols. Your swag should somehow point back to you and your product/service. For example, a bathtub fitter could give out funky scrub brushes or rubber duckies imprinted with their logo when a client has a bathtub installed. Present photo mugs to those who buy your upscale coffee machine.

6. **Consumable notepad or non-consumable pen set?** A consumable item is acceptable, but better if it has a long shelf-life. I seem to have a continuous supply of notepads from realtors, but some of them waste over half the paper with their logo. I tend to use the back of these rather than the front, which defeats the purpose. Also, every time a new one with a massive advert arrives, I think of that person as wasteful, not something I would want to be known for. While non-consumables seem practical, a person can only use so many keychains, letter openers or mugs. The extras - the less attractive ones for sure - will be tossed in the collect-

all drawer never to be looked at or touched again. Think attractive and useful so that your branded gift will be handled on a daily basis.

7. **How does your token reflect on your company?** If your gift is cheap, gimmicky or unsuitable for your market, it will reflect poorly. Choose your items carefully. Have a wide range of people - clients, family and friends - check it out before you buy it. You may love that quirky nose hair twizzler with your logo on the side, but your staff might gag at the very idea of giving it to someone.

Here are a few ideas to jump-start your creative thinking process:

1. Offer free checklists to clients who stop by. Have them laminated with a magnetic strip on the back so they can be kept on the fridge:

    - A travel agency could print up a checklist of essentials to procure/pack before the big vacation
    - A real estate agent could have a checklist of places to send a change of address or a list of local moving companies that are trustworthy and reasonably priced
    - A printing company could have a checklist for designing the perfect business card

2. Is there a special occasion your client is celebrating? A sunny bouquet of flowers or a box of gourmet chocolates with a handwritten note is always welcome.

3. Have you read a good book that a client would benefit from? Send them a copy. Send them *your* copy with a note inside referring them to the sections that reminded you of them. Only do this if it's a positive reminder. Never send someone a book in order to cure them of something. I hope that goes without saying, but you never know.

A Little Gift to Remember Me By

4. Hand out roses on Mother's Day and maybe "Dad's Root Beer" (Dad.TheNectarEffect.com) on Father's Day. Don't worry if people are parents or not, just give the gifts to the appropriate adult who walks in. Perhaps you could have a fun toy for kids, as well: mini-frisbees, bouncy rubber balls, funny sunglasses, etc.

Dad's Root Beer

5. Send gifts when a client signs up with you. It would be ideal if you could come up with something that was your signature item that all new clients received. Something very special. If you don't want to fuss, most people like to receive unexpected treats, like the previously mentioned brownies.

6. If you design a new website for a client, give them a business card template to match at no extra charge.

7. A real-estate company could work hand in hand with a cleaning company and offer a complete, professional home cleaning to both sellers and buyers instead of a fruit basket or bouquet of flowers. This would also make a much appreciated gift amongst the new parents on your client list.

8. Are your clients young families? A restaurant gift certificate would be well-received as most people can't afford both a sitter and a dinner out. Or, be even more creative, and offer them a dinner evening in their own home by hiring a personal chef (here in Calgary, my favourite personal chef is Chef Giuseppe: Chef.TheNectarEffect.com)

9. Offer gift cards for purchase and then give the purchaser a 20% off coupon to come back and shop with whomever they're giving the gift card to - a double whammy!

10. Come up with a clever and affordable gift idea for your clients for Christmas. A tasteful, personalized ornament is

a gift that could be cherished for years to come as long as it doesn't have your logo fouling the artwork on the front. The back should be sufficient, especially if the ornament is exquisite.

11. Make a donation to a customer's favourite charity.
12. Give them a discount on one of their monthly bills "just because". Do this randomly with each of your clients.
13. If you're a B2B business, offer your clients free advertising, a free press release or some other way to get the word out for their business. Keep your name well out of it.
14. Create a daily calendar with inspirational quotes surrounding your field of expertise that your clients may be encouraged every day of the year.

You can build your email list with gifts, too. Use a free product to encourage your prospects to leave their name and email address. Here are some ideas to try:

1. **A report** - Provide an analysis on the current state of the industry you represent, or provide a list of possible time-saving uses for your product/service.
2. **An interview** - Periodically interview the experts in your industry and offer these recordings as a free download for your subscribers.
3. **A series of videos** - create a series of how-to videos for your customers to answer their questions and familiarize them with you and the product.
4. **A free teleseminar or a webinar** -teach your clients how to pick up a new skill by recording it and then providing it as a freebie.
5. **An audio recording** - make a recording of yourself sharing key information about your business or product

A Little Gift to Remember Me By

Whatever extra value you offer, it must be of high quality and focused in its purpose so that what your client receives will be noted and appreciated. Don't just throw something together with little thought. Craft your gift/giveaway with care, consideration, and with your *client's* best interests in mind to create wonderful inspiration for referrals.

Tips for getting started right away:

1. Work at designing one thing to give away on your website to build your list
2. Brainstorm with a promotions company (I recommend Swag.TheNectarEffect.com) to create a unique gift as a giveaway for your business to build brand recognition and decide the best way for you to use this most effectively as a part of your overall marketing strategy.

Creating a Stir Through Events

Several years ago my church put on a local fun fair with live music, arcade games and bouncy castles. We took over the local community centre and the large piece of property around it. It was festive and free of charge and was used to bless the community the church was located in, as well as to improve the church's profile. The event was packed all day. I ran one of the bouncy castles and I kept having people say "I'm sorry, but I can't find the place to buy tickets." I took great pleasure in telling them the event was a gift from my church to this community and that there was no charge, religious soliciting, or obligation. The look on their faces was priceless. The kudos my church received were innumerable and it was a wonderful example of branding.

The definition for Event Marketing, according to the Google Dictionary is:

> *a promotional strategy linking a company to a special event (sponsorship of a sports competition, festival, etc.) to support corporate objectives.*

If you're a small business wanting to increase exposure, creating or participating in an event is something you'll want to try. Do consider from the beginning, that an event can be an expensive endeavor that will require much thought and planning on your part to make it come to life. It can be anything from a local barbecue to a national seminar; it all depends on your budget and your objectives.

The Nectar Effect

There are some common types of events - workshops, seminars, partnering with charities, trade shows, concerts - and there are some more involved ideas where a whole, multi-faceted event is pulled together combining any or all of the above. You can choose to just participate or actually set the whole thing up yourself. It can be a one-business show or it can involve several businesses all coming together under one roof, enabling you to create a much larger splash for a more affordable fee.

The key to a successful event is, once again, thinking about what your ideal client needs. What is the most meaningful occasion you can create that fits the profile of your ideal client? Think of a theme and participate in an existing event or build a specific event around that concept. Some example of this are as follows:

- You have a nutrition/weight loss product and you wish to build an event around the importance of having a fit, strong body for health and longevity. You could sponsor a health and fitness expo by inviting people in the industry such as holistic practitioners, chiropractors, massage therapists, fitness clubs, personal trainers, sports clothing retail stores, etc. to offer workshops/seminars in addition to participating in a mini trade show.

- You are a real-estate agent who wants to show care for the community you serve. Stage an event to raise funds for a new community centre or playground or organize and sponsor an event to support a local non-profit organization. Or you could organize a home-staging workshop so people can prepare their homes for a quicker sale.

- As a financial planner you could ask your contacts in the field to do a workshop on various aspects of money management, such as budgeting, RRSP's, the basics of the stock market, investing in mutual funds, etc.

Creating a Stir Through Events

Whatever you decide, your event needs to place you as the expert in your field, the one people will call on when they need help in the area you do business in. As the planner, you control the size and scheduling and can create intimate opportunities, such as coffee times, mixers or open forums to connect with your target market and find out what it is they really need and want from you. The feedback you gain might give you some great ideas for new products and services.

If you can manage it, host a workshop or event that brings in a big name who can teach you and your staff, colleagues and clients about what's new and upcoming in your area. You benefit by staying on the cutting edge while sharing the costs with the attendees.

Don't let yourself get sucked into the idea that an event has to be large and bodacious to have an effect. Even the smallest kindnesses can generate an impact, and an intimate gathering can be just as powerful - if not more so - than a big fancy occasion.

Here are some ideas you can mull over for your business:

1. Challenge your neighbors to join you as you clean up the community and invite participants back for refreshments
2. Sponsor or co-sponsor the local baseball/ hockey/soccer team
3. Launch a charity fundraiser
4. Offer your services free of charge for an underprivileged group in your neighborhood on a specific day (a day of free tune-ups for single moms, free financial advice or consult/ analysis for new business owners, free childcare and fitness classes for young moms, etc.)
5. Offer to teach one or two of the classes in the Life-Skills course in your local high school, or offer a workshop in the local library or Chamber of Commerce.

6. Set up a craft fair/art show for local artists. If you are an artisan, you can feature your works as the promoter of the event. If you support artists (by marketing them or by selling craft supplies, for example) you could use the event to reconnect with them and showcase their talents.

7. In a similar vein, stage a home shopping party in the community centre with different products and organizations represented.

8. Create a local contest that encourages calling on your ideal prospects to showcase their talents/skills.

9. Create a specialized networking group. You can focus on women in business, network marketing, local businesses, artists, etc. Have regular continuing education seminars for members.

10. Offer your services/products as give-aways in recurring local events, such as music, culture and performing arts festivals.

11. If your community is hosting an event, volunteering is an easy way to get to know new people. Everyone is worth meeting, even if they aren't your ideal client, they may know of someone who could use your product/service. Work for the cause with cheerfulness and stamina and your presence and person will be remembered in a positive way.

12. Donate a certain percentage of all your revenue to a worthy cause during a particular month. Host a contest with a substantial prize for the person who refers the most business to you in that month. Praise the prize winner at the close of the contest and share your total contribution as a result of your clients' efforts to aide your giving.

13. Produce a practical series of articles and publish them monthly in the local community newspaper. Cover topics such as health and fitness, organization, money saving

and budgeting, marketing of home-based businesses, etc., information that we all need to go about our lives. Don't be temped to conclude them them with a sales pitch or your readership will fall like a stone. Your product or service shouldn't even be mentioned except in your author bio.

14. Host a Customer Appreciation Day and provide prizes, giveaways, contests, food, and fun activities that will create a positive, supportive impression of your business. Use your storefront or your local community centre.

Whatever you decide, keep your customer in mind and see if you can pull something together that will be helpful, enriching and uplifting.

If you are not comfortable with groups of people, seek out your local Toastmasters (TM.TheNectarEffect.com). Learn and practice public speaking skills while you share about your business in your speeches. Your fellow presenters will be sure to heckle you if you're obnoxiously pushing your wares. However, they will also help you hone your presentation, making it more concise and effective.

Toastmasters

Steps for setting up a great event:

1. Choose the kind of event you want to stage.//
2. Decide what it is you want to accomplish. Write your goals down in detail. Be outrageous. You can pare down later. Dream big.
3. Find the people you need to help you out - sponsors, joint-venture partners, community leaders, etc. Try to involve different age groups in your community. Pay a group of teenagers to help you set up and take down. Ask for baking donations from parents and seniors.

4. Decide who your target market is and where/how you'll most likely be able to reach them. Find other businesses who cater in a non-competing way to this group and work together.
5. Prepare a budget.
6. Choose your date, time, and location.
7. Figure out how many people you can comfortably accommodate.
8. Create a planning calendar and determine the periodic deadlines you will need to meet to get everything done in good time.
9. Arrange for special guests.
10. Decide on decorations and equipment and begin to gather supplies.
11. Create your marketing plan. Include online and offline marketing. Everyone involved in the planning should be advertising, as well.

Of course, we've only been dealing with location-based events in this chapter, but it's also possible to create fun online events too. You can do a webinar, a blogging festival with complimentary businesses, a video contest, or a social media contest.

Survey Monkey

Once you've decided on an event, get excited. Talk about your event to whomever will listen. Get your family and friends involved and be so enthusiastic that it's contagious. Video document the process and make up a musical montage to close the event showing all the people it took to make it happen. Thank everyone from co-creators to volunteers to clients verbally and in writing. Send out your thank you cards, including photos and testimonials soon after the party's completion. In the card, direct them to the online survey you created to help you measure the overall success. SurveyMonkey (Survey.TheNectarEffect.com) is a good resource for this.

Tips for getting started right away:

1. Have a lunch meeting and tap your team for 10–12 ways to bless and encourage your clients both online and offline.
2. Choose the ones that you believe are the top 3–4 and decide their order of priority.
3. Set a deadline for getting the most profitable idea up and running.

Trade Show Tactics

A few months ago I participated in a thought-provoking thread about trade shows on my LinkedIn account. People were complaining that they had invested a great deal of money in their booth and display to come away not having made a single sale.

The discussion started because of a small business trade show that I attended as a spectator rather than an exhibitor. It was educational to be able to observe the show in person and hear the comments afterward. My observations are as follows:

1. At the exhibit itself, no single booth jumped out at me. There was nothing to set any one booth apart from any other. I didn't sense any special energy in the room and nothing eventful happening at any particular location. It was all product related and nothing really grabbed my attention or piqued my curiosity.

2. Almost everyone had a sign-up for a free draw. Of course, I put my name in all of them and, not only did I *not* win, but a mere two of the exhibitors contacted me post-show and none of them did anything more than send me a single template email.

3. There were three exhibitors I had positive discussions with who had products I was interested in. In each case, I left my card with my contact information and asked them to call me to set up an appointment. Not one of them called me. Allow

me to restate, that I was *interested in putting my money down on their product.* I had my information ready to give them. Not one followed up.

It's quite pricey to participate in a trade show and as small business owners we can't afford to waste that investment. Because of this, I've gathered a handful of helpful hints to make sure your next show is a dazzling success.

Before the show

1. **What is the Nectar, the sweet seed of your business?** You need to focus on the one unforgettable attribute you want to communicate when you're there. You might have a dozen strong selling points, but choose one flagship idea for the show and build your presentation around that. A trade show is no different from a carnival; the lights, the noise, the colourful gewgaws, the crowds of consumers, the vendors keen on snagging a sale. This is what you're up against. Whatever you're presenting had better be attractive, remarkable and memorable or you and yours will get lost in the pyscho-shuffle and spat out the other end with a bag full of mini donuts and a divot in your dwindling bank account.

2. **Know why you're there**. Is it to create awareness? Sell product? Is it to collect leads? Book appointments? Of course, ideally, we want all of the above to happen, but just like with our intuitive client, we need to laser our efforts for a single outcome, so we don't waste time, energy or money. Defining one clear purpose for being there will help you measure whether or not it was a successful show. Even if you fall short of a goal, you have a yardstick to go by for the next event.

3. **Prep your staff**. If you have people manning the booth for you, make sure everyone understands the goals, has a thorough working knowledge of the service/product, and

can articulate the party line with accuracy and enthusiasm. Let them know they are not to be slumped over in the booth chomping on popcorn or playing on their phones. Their shifts should be short enough that a high energy level may be maintained in the booth at all times.

4. **Read the Small Print.** Make sure you're fully aware of what is permitted and supplied. Check this list repeatedly to make sure you're not breaking any rules with your presentation.

5. **Plan the outcome.** Know that there are four things your exhibit needs to do to be successful. Arrive at your booth with your strategy mapped out in a concrete way.

- **Attract.** You may be competing with 20 booths or 2000. How are you going to make yourself known? What kind of presentation will draw your ideal client to you? Others may walk by disinterested, but you want your target market to notice the Nectar and make a beeline.

- **Engage.** When your target prospect has approached your booth, how are you going to entice them? Here are three possiblities:
  - Prize draws
  - Giveaways
  - On-site activities like a product demonstration, seminar, game, computer presentation. Give a five minute infomercial at your booth every hour on the hour. Don't sell, educate.

- **Capture.** The prize draw should capture as much information as a patron is willing to share, but at the minimum, their name and email address. Also include a box on this slip asking if they'd be interested in receiving your newsletter (and DON'T put them on your list unless they've checked this, unless you want to be hit with a spam complaint!)

The process of moving hot prospects forward smoothly and efficiently should be in place and the steps followed by everyone: have your appointment calendar, contracts, payment options and product to hand.

- **Follow up.** Your trade show budget should include funds for stellar followup. Make it your first priority to add those who gave you permission into your newsletter. When their first copy goes out, write a note on it thanking them for their interest. Anyone who requested specific information should receive their mail-out within the week and if anyone wanted to put their money down on something they should receive a call during office hours the next business day. Send everyone who was gracious enough to provide you with their contact information a physical card thanking them for stopping by. Remember, 80% of sales are made on the 5th-12th contact, which means you should have a way of popping in to say hi to your new contacts at least 12 times over the next few months. Every point of connection should have cumulative value visible to your prospect.

6. **Check It Out**. Before you sign up for a trade show, it's a good idea to attend one by the hosting organization first. You will need to know who your competition is likely to be and how they are attracting, engaging, capturing and following up. Chat with the vendors there to find out what's great and not-so-great about working that particular trade show. Grill them for their experienced advice!

7. **Know Your Client.** Who is your ideal client? Do your homework; know your target market, what they want, and how to engage them. The trade show you're considering should be geared to that person.

8. **Design your Booth.** Think about the size and uniqueness of your display booth. Before you spend hundreds of dollars

on this, check into the booth specifications for the show beforehand. I spoke to one woman who had spent $200 on a special banner/header for her booth only to find out she wasn't allowed to use it. You may want to bring portable light fixtures with you on set-up day. Some booths end up being very dark due to their placement. If people can't see you, they won't stop.

Avoid putting a table across the front of your area. This blocks traffic and gives a "closed" impression. Instead, use several small tables of varied heights along the back of the space with each one featuring different items to create visual interest. This invites people in.

You might even want to have a corner set aside for children with crayons, coloring books, stickers, etc. so they're entertained while their parents are talking. Having someone blow bubbles for young children in your booth is also a good idea as long as they're not too copious and disruptive to the booths around you.

Include fresh flowers and chocolates in your display.

9. **Invite Your Market**. Send a personalized invitation by mail to your current clients and any prospects you have, inviting them to bring a friend and stop by for a chance to win a prize. Perhaps you can include an incentive like two free tickets to the show or some on-site meal vouchers in your invitation.

- Use social media including blogging to create some buzz around your exhibit beforehand, so people come to the show looking for you.

- Put an ad in the local paper concerning the trade show listing the reasons people will want to stop by your booth for a visit.

- Do something extraordinary. Jen sterling of Red Thinking (Red.TheNectarEffect.com) shares this story of how she thought ahead for a client and made their trade show experience a positive one:

People attending trade shows will often buzz through and then take off for the hotel pool. Get their attention before they ever arrive so that they seek YOU out. We had a client whose trade show theme was Hawaii. We packaged up pineapples in bags with their logo screened on it. We attached a funny little brochure about the "Ten Things to do with Your Pineapple" and mailed them off in advance of the show.

Red Thinking

They had NEVER before received so many visitors to their booth. The feedback was fantastic.

10. **Brand your business.** Make sure everyone in the booth is easily identified as being part of your team with either a uniform, similar shirts with your business name branded in a small logo on the right hand side or bright, plucky chicken costumes (yeah, just kidding on that last one, unless you're a chicken farm or something...)

11. **Pay Attention to the details.** Are you aware of all the guidelines and restrictions? Do you know the dimensions of the space? Do you have tables? Table cloths? Do you need a power source and is there a nearby electrical outlet? Will the lighting be sufficient?

12. **Make it professional.** Make sure your graphics don't look like they were printed off your computer that morning and colored inside the lines by your five-year-old. If you want to be viewed as a bona fide business and not a lemonade stand, use professional graphics.

13. **Prepare a FAQ sheet.** Review all your protocols with your employees before going in. Frequently asked questions - a list that should be easy to compile based on feedback from your existing customers - should be handled by all staff in a consistent, clear manner. Your staff should also be briefed as to how to handle questions they can't answer. If you are not available to offer your expertise, this would be a great opportunity to capture contact information and provide the answer to the inquiring party as soon as possible during or after the show.

14. **Contact collection.** There are several options, but all are best attached to a draw as people are more willing to cough up their contact info if there is a chance they might win something they can use. Here are some ideas for capturing their information:

    - A business card scanner
    - A fish bowl to collect business cards
    - A sign-up sheet or entry form.

      Ask for everything - name, home and cell phone numbers, address, etc. but let them decide what to fill in. Specify on the form or on nearby signage that full name and email address are required to enter the draw.

15. **Pick a great spot.** If you are able to choose where your booth will be at the time of registration, do so. The ends of the middle rows are the best choice, as well as near the doors.

16. **Gather supplies**. Be prepared with things like additional lighting, table cloths, display stands, a basic tool kit, hooks, duct tape, extension cords, sewing kit, stain remover, first aid kit, pain relief tablets, full water bottles, breath mints, wipes, paper towel and a back up of everything you need just in case.

17. **Choose your giveaways**. Some great giveaways are;
    - Bottled water with your business label on the front
    - Themed chocolates with your logo on the wrapping. I had a friend in the finance industry who gave away chocolates in the shape of dollar signs, wrapped in cellophane bags with her business card tied to the top. Very memorable, as chocolate always is!
    - Put your information on cans of energy drinks.
    - Hand out bright, eco-friendly bags for the attendees to put their pamphlets and samples in as they walk through the show.
    - Hand out screen cleaners for their portable devices, mini hand sanitizer bottles or lip balm branded by you.
    - Have balloons with your logo made to give out to the kids.

All of these could be distributed away from your booth in another part of the show along with an invitation to stop by your booth for additional goodies and/or the draw. This way people have a connection with you before they even get to your show location.

Nowadays, most people appreciate gifts that are environmentally friendly. My Honda dealer hands out seed packets instead of brochures. The seed packets have a link to their website. This is something to consider when coming up with giveaways, as well as when deciding what paper you will pass out. As far as paper products go, brochures are standard fodder for the recycling bin. A coupon, a humorous calendar or lists of tips to ease everyday living may have a longer shelf-life than your glossy flyer. If they have little or no value to the customer they may be taken out of politeness and tossed at home. They will need to be useful enough to accomplish your intended purpose of getting you in the door of their home and then allowing you to become a household name.

During the Show

1. Your support staff must be clean and well-groomed. They must be bright, cheerful and competent. There must be no yawning, gum chewing, book reading, hand-held game playing, cell phone addiction, and above all, no whining or bickering allowed. They need to be as focused and excited as you are to produce a successful show.

2. Draw the crowd to you by having a trendy magician or actor in a funny costume walk around with an invitation to enter your draw.

3. Approach other booths that have a complimentary offering and ask to exchange referrals: *Hey, if you like my hand-razored spandex body glove you might also like Tiffany's Extra Sparkle Perty Pink Complexion Powder. Give her some love at booth 97 in aisle 3. Tell her Ashley sent you.* Proceed to give them one of Tiffany's cards and supplying directions to her temporary abode. Talk to those you network with, those businesses you have referred to in the past and see who is planning to attend the show and if they would be willing to set up a reciprocal marketing campaign for the event and share the costs and the leads.

4. Incorporate the sense of smell into your presentation. If you're in health and wellness, try using lavender or vanilla. scents that mimic baked goods (such as an "apple pie" candle) bring back memories of comfort. (*Note: Be careful here to use natural scents rather than chemical scents, as people are often very sensitive to these, and will avoid your booth if the smell makes them uncomfortable.*)

If you have cooking utensils and will be demonstrating their use, prepare something that has a delicious aroma strong enough to pervade a wide radius. Brew a pungent pot of coffee or tea and serve a warm cup to your clients. Have an old-fashioned popcorn machine churning out free popcorn. Again, check the rules before you spend the money to set this up. Some shows won't allow you to offer food at your booth.

5. Create a "treasure hunt" with QR codes. Have a handful of people wearing t-shirts, each with a different QR code, wander around the exhibit inviting people to scan them for a prize. Let each one be a clue. They need all 5, or whatever number you choose, to win a prize at your booth.

You could also design this with punch cards and different die cutters. so that people go around and gather the different punches, and then enter their ballot into the draw once they've collected them all.

6. Ask a Question to Passersby - Have a compelling question ready to ask people as they walk by. For example:

- "Hello! Do you want to boost your energy while exploring the exhibit? " Offer an energy/health drink sample.

- "Hello, you look terrific! Would you like to look 10 years younger before you go home?" Offer a free facial.

- "Hello! Are you a pet lover? Would you like a unique gift for that special pet in your life?" Offer an individually packaged treat.

7. Contain the mess. Manage your booth's image as products are sold. Fliers and promotional material get picked up leaving holes and/or messy piles behind when traffic gets heavy. Have someone at your booth whose sole purpose it is to keep your area clean, tidy, organized and restocked at all times.

8. Take Pictures. Have someone snapping photos throughout the day. After the show, send all your leads an email inviting them to view a collage on an attractive page linked to your website.

After the Show

Follow up, follow up, follow up. See chapter 8 for my personal system of follow up for some ideas, and add your newsletter for anyone who gave you permission to put them on your subscribers list. Add all new contacts to your database, file their cards and connect with each one in as many places as you can online: follow them on Twitter, set up a blog feed for their blog, connect with them on LinkedIn and YouTube and Google+, and request them as a friend on Facebook or invite them to like your page and do the same for them.

It could take up to 12 months of regular, value-added contact to create a purchase. How are you going to nurture your client long enough to get there? How many different ways can you create contact that will add value and build relationship? How will you sustain the relationship to keep a loyal client?

You will have many people coming by who just want the freebie. Here are some ideas separating the opportunists from future clients:

1. Tailor giveaways to suit your target market. Offer a discount coupon, a month's free service, a complimentary business analysis and consult. Avoid proffering the latest trending electronic gadget or you may find yourself rewarding your competitor's clients.

2. Have a special gift for those with whom you strike up a meaningful conversation about your business. Keep these leads separate. They're the ones you'll do the most vigorous follow up with. You might set up different follow up campaigns for different people:

- One for anyone who stopped by and signed up for something
- One for those who showed interest and with whom you offered your second offering (see point 2)
- Those who expressed interest in moving forward.

Tips for getting started today:

1. Conduct research on trade shows going on in your area and attend as many as you're able to, for the purpose of gathering ideas. Screen the possibilities for all aspects of your business from display ideas and graphics to marketing and giveaways, etc.
2. Choose one or two shows and scrutinize them. How do they present themselves? How much competition is there in your industry and who are they? Check out their follow up practices by leaving your personal contact info.
3. Start formulating a plan for your own exhibit the following year.

Conclusion

You've finished! You're clean, polished, polite, kind, compassionate and prepared to release your Nectar into the air around you. Hopefully, reading this book was fun, engaging and inspiring. Hopefully there were at least a handful of ideas in here that will help you move your business forward without sucking up all your rare, free time. Hopefully, the book enabled you to come up with several ideas of your own. Thank you for reading.

Remember, your business is more about you than about your product. It's more about your character and personality than your marketing plan - though hear me when I say that both of these are also important. Of course, you need to have a valuable product or service and you need to know where you're going in order to figure out how to get there!

Be yourself; your gentle, genuine, captivating, self; help, give, serve and grow. Draw out the sweetness in others, because it's there, waiting to be extracted. Bloom wherever you are; grace that place and you'll be visited there in that luminous plot of earth again and again. They'll come for the Nectar.

I'd love to hear how this book is helping you build a better business. I'd consider using your stories as conversation starters on my blog (with a link back to your business, of

Send Me an Email!

course!) and possibly in a future book. Please email your stories to info@hotspotsocialmedia.com.

The competition is fierce out there! If you found this book in any way helpful, a review on Amazon would help my little book shine through the noise, and I'd be so very grateful.

Acknowledgements

Darlene:

For Polly: Thank you for adding joy and sunshine to my often dusty words and for working perfectly unreasonable hours to get this finished on time. Thanks for making me laugh out loud and helping me believe in this vision.

For Alice: what a tireless, patient editor you are! I am so very grateful for all the wonderful advice, corrections, and gentle scolding. I think we were both surprised at how many places quotation marks DIDN'T belong!

For Mom and Dad: I won't live long enough to pay you back for the hassle, but I appreciate the fact that you still love me. Thanks for raising me in an environment of possibility and dreaming and for not giving up on me when it looked bleak.

For Debbie, Lynda, and Logan: it's not always been an easy journey with this sister of yours. Thank you for your patience and for not rolling your eyes too often or too obviously.

For Simon: So glad you're my son! Thanks for fixing Polly's computer at the zero hour, for keeping mine from seizing up, for making sure there were regular tea breaks, and for keeping a steady supply of TV reruns ready for those moments when my poor brain could no longer formulate a reasonable thought.

For Tina: So glad you're my daughter! Thanks for keeping the house under control, for using this time to hone your cooking skills and for making sure we didn't starve to death, for coming down and resting your chin on my shoulder at regular intervals to remind me that I was, after all, first and foremost a mom, and for putting up with all the disjointed conversation topics coming out of my mouth.

For Tom - I cannot believe I was lucky enough to be chosen by you! You are, indeed, the wind beneath my wings. Bless you for supporting me, putting up with my crazy schemes, cooking your own dinner, keeping the dishwasher running, and most of all, for letting me stay.

For Jesus - thank you for making me quirky. It's taken a long time to accept it, but the journey has been worth it all!

Polly:

For Darlene: Your inclusion of me in this project was an unexpected gift at a difficult time. Your friendship was an unexpected gift I will cherish for the rest of my life. I love you, my sister and friend.

For my parents: Ron and Sharon Mayforth: Look at me, Mom and Dad. I wrote me a book! Thank you for your faithful love, encouragement and support. I wouldn't be who I am on this day if it wasn't for you. I love you.

For my precious children: Grace, Timothy and Rose. My goal as your mother, besides loving you, laughing with you and bugging you, is to help you find your passion and pursue it to its glorious fruition. I love you.

For Myron Krause: My best friend and the one who has always been there when I looked beside me. You've been my rock and my shelter. Thank you. I love you.

For God: Who laughs with me and at me whenever I think things are impossible. We do loads of laughing together, don't we?

About the Authors

Darlene Hull is the founder and president of HotSpot Social Media, an energetic, enthusiastic, creative social media force that believes in a "Back To Basics Step By Step" process for highly effective, highly efficient, painless and profitable social media. (HotSpotSocialMedia.com)

When not on social media, Darlene is a barefoot endurance walker, a speaker, teacher, author, professional musician and worship leader. She takes her tea and chocolate intravenously.

Darlene currently resides in Calgary, Alberta with her husband and their two adult children who also work with with her in the family social media business.

Polly Mayforth Krause is a wordsmith through and through, as well as a voice-over artist. She has a wry sense of humour and takes great joy in crafting communication that entices and entertains.

Polly lives not far from the Canadian Rocky Mountains in Lethbridge, Alberta, Canada, with her husband and 3 children. She is is humbled and grateful to reside in such a magnificent place.

Made in the USA
Charleston, SC
08 February 2015